SUPERSTARS OF

EURO 2000

This is a Parragon Book
First published in 2000

Parragon
Queen Street House
4 Queen Street
Bath BA1 1HE, UK

Produced by International Publishing Associates

Words: Paul Fry
Design: Rob Benson

ISBN: 0-75253-935-3

CONTENTS

Heroic England were the class of '96

The NEARLY MEN

GAZZA KISS: Sheringham gets a Gascoigne hug after scoring against Holland.

FOOTBALL'S COMING HOME, sang the nation four years ago as the heroic efforts of Terry Venables' men restored the smile to the face of English football.

Euro96 came to England... and England almost came to conquer.

They were denied only after a penalty shoot-out in the semi-final with Germany, just as they had been six years earlier in a World Cup semi-final in Italy.

Shearer, Sheringham and company bowed out with dignity and pride, leaving fabulous memories to savour, including a momentous 4-1 victory over Holland. A new passion abounded 30 years after Moore, Hurst, Peters, Charlton and Co. became legends by winning the World Cup.

All in all, Euro96 went off famously, with memories of a hooligan past consigned to history.

England, as hosts, did not have their familiar qualifying struggle. Scotland did, but clung on behind Russia to join the party – drawn in the same group as the Auld Enemy!

SHEAR GENIUS: A salute from Shearer after another goal against the Dutch.

But that small matter had to wait. England opened at Wembley with an Alan Shearer goal but Switzerland spoiled the day with a late penalty equaliser.

Meanwhile, the Tartan Army celebrated a gallant 0-0 draw against Holland before heading for Wembley. Shearer's early strike silenced the Scots until they won a penalty. Scottish hearts sank when captain Gary McAllister's kick was beaten away by David Seaman and then a touch of genius by Paul Gascoigne sealed the win. Gazza flicked the ball over Colin Hendry's head before volleying past Andy Goram. It was one of the greatest goals Wembley had ever seen.

A draw would have suited both England and Holland from their final group clash. But the Dutch reckoned without one of England's finest displays, in which the brilliantly unpredictable Gascoigne again excelled. Teddy Sheringham and Shearer put on their party pieces, and, but for Patrick Kluivert's late consolation goal (to make it 4-1), the Scots would have made the quarter-finals along with England. Instead, Holland went forward on goal difference.

France and Croatia, along with a youthful Portugal, made it a memorable tournament full of attacking football to savour. Davor Suker's wonderful chip from the half-way line, which almost beat Schmeichel, provided one of the highlights of the tournament. And the Czech, Karel Poborsky, earned a transfer to Manchester United with his solo run and delicate chipped finish against Portugal.

Italy were sneaking into the last eight until German keeper Andy Koepke, lucky not to be sent off for felling Pierluigi Casiraghi, saved a penalty from Gianfranco Zola. The Czech Republic's 3-3 draw with Russia meant an early exit for the Italians and a place in the knockout stage for themselves.

STU-PENDOUS: A lion's roar from Pearce after his penalty against Spain.

The quarter-finals were largely tame, England's clash with Spain excepted. The Spaniards, wrongly as TV replays proved, had a goal ruled out for offside and had two penalty claims turned down at an expectant Wembley. Neither side could find the Golden Goal that would have cut short extra-time, so it went to penalties.

Defender Stuart Pearce famously rifled one home to make amends for his 1990 World Cup semi-final miss and then Seaman saved decisively from Miguel Nadal to book a date with the Germans, who had survived a battering from Croatia.

‘Alan Shearer gave England a dream start’

It needed penalties to separate the Czechs from floundering France in the semi-finals. But Wembley again took centre stage as England looked to avenge Italia90’s disappointment of a penalties defeat by the Germans. It was close to call, but little could anyone know that the same agonies were to be endured.

The irrepressible Shearer gave England a dream start with a goal – his fifth of the tournament – after just three minutes. Stefan Kuntz levelled. There were precious few openings until Darren Anderton was inches from a glorious Golden Goal in extra-time.

So it was penalties – again! Neither side faltered and the score was locked at 5-5. Then the otherwise faultless Gareth Southgate’s tame effort was saved by Koepke and Andy Moller scored to win a hugely emotional tie. Southgate’s reward was to feature in a pizza commercial with a bag over his head!

The Germans’ famed resilience showed again in the final against the Czech Republic, whose progress had been almost unnoticed. Patrik Berger’s 59th-minute penalty was saluted at Wembley by 65,000 Englishmen, all honorary Czechs for the night. But they suffered yet again at the hands of the Germans, as Oliver Bierhoff struck twice, including the Golden Goal winner four minutes into extra-time. It was ‘Two Biers and One Berger’, as one headline recorded the next day.

Terry Venables signed off as England boss by collecting the Fair Play award, handing over the reins to Glenn Hoddle.

The prize was small consolation. But Euro96’s legacy will be its success in helping secure another World Cup finals for the home of football. Then that rousing ‘Three Lions’ song will need a bit of updating...

POISONED PEN: Southgate after missing his spot kick against Germany.

‘Like the World Cup, it was invented by a Frenchman’

The World Cup was almost 30 years old when the countries of Europe – well, 17 of them – got together to kick-off their own nations' championship.

Like the World Cup, dreamt up by Jules Rimet, the European Nations' Cup was the brainchild of a Frenchman. Henri Delaunay was secretary of the French Football Federation but died before the first competition got under way in 1958. However, the magnificent silver trophy, lifted four years ago by the German striking legend Jurgen Klinsmann, still bears Delaunay's name.

There had been small tournaments throughout the continent. England, Scotland, Northern Ireland and Wales competed in the British Championship, which began in 1883. The Scandinavian countries, Sweden, Norway, Denmark and Finland, set up their own event in 1924. Three years later, the Central European championship – later known rather grandly as 'the Europe Cup' – began, with Austria, Italy, Switzerland, Hungary and Czechoslovakia competing.

In 1960, the Soviet Union beat Yugoslavia in front of just 18,000 in Paris to win the first final, after a four-team final phase. It was 20 years before the competition got a mini World Cup-style finals tournament.

JURGEN TO WIN: Klinsmann urges on his team-mates after scoring against Russia on the way to the 1996 final.

FRENCH MUSTARD: Michel Platini was too hot to hold in 1984.

And it was only in 1984, when the great French team led by Michel Platini won on home soil, that the event gained the recognition that Real Madrid brought to the Champion Clubs' Cup in the Fifties.

Spain made full use of home advantage when they beat the Soviets in 1964 in Madrid, for their only success in a major competition to date.

Four years later, with World champions England expected to do well, there were eight qualifying groups and England battled past Northern Ireland, Scotland and Wales to reach the quarter-finals.

There was one major embarrassing hiccup along the way, though – England's famous 3-2 Wembley defeat by the Scots, less than a year after winning the World Cup. Geoff Hurst, who scored six goals in the campaign, was on target for Sir Alf Ramsey's heroes. But Denis Law, Bobby Lennox and Jim McCalliog struck the goals that secured a victory that the Scots still cherish today.

In the knockout phase, England had two tough encounters with Spain, the reigning European champions. England won a tight first leg at Wembley thanks to a goal by Bobby Charlton. But they had to show their true pedigree in a 2-1 win in Madrid in front of 120,000 at the Bernabeu Stadium with Hurst and Martin Peters grabbing the vital goals.

The semi-final in Florence was a bruiser. Yugoslavia seemed intent on intimidating England, and Tottenham's Alan Mullery was harshly sent off – the first ever England international player to be dismissed. Dragan Dzajic scored the only goal and England were left to beat Russia three days later in Rome, 2-0, to finish third – their best ever achievement in the competition.

Italy needed a replay to overcome the rugged Yugoslavs, after making five changes to their side for the second match. The majority of that team would go on to face arguably the best national side ever, the Brazil of Pele, Jairzinho and Carlos Alberto, in the World Cup two years later.

'SWEDES 2

GERD AS GOLD: Muller's goals saw Germany win in 1972.

The Russians reached their third final in four attempts but 1972 found the Germans on the rise to new peaks. Gerd Muller, Germany's goal predator extraordinary, scored twice in a 3-0 win in Brussels. Muller had scored in a 3-1 quarter-final first-leg victory against England at Wembley, dominated by midfield general Gunter Netzer. A routine 0-0 draw in the return sufficed for the Germans, and another Muller double saw off Belgium to book their place in the final.

Four years later, West Germany reached the final again, this time against Czechoslovakia, who had qualified from England's group despite losing 3-0 at Wembley. Successive draws with Portugal had undermined England's hopes and Wales were the only home qualifiers, losing 2-0 and drawing at home 1-1 with Yugoslavia in the quarter-finals.

Italy and France also failed to reach the finals, where the 1974 World Cup finalists Holland and West Germany seemed sure to collide again.

However, the Czechs beat Holland in extra-time and a hat-trick by substitute Dieter Muller (no relation to Gerd) helped the Germans beat Yugoslavia 4-2 in Belgrade.

The final is remembered most for its penalty shoot-out climax – the first to settle a major competition. And this one had a twist. The sides had been deadlocked at 2-2 after extra-time and the holders were thankful, having trailed 2-0, only to tie it up with a minute remaining.

In the shoot-out, Uli Hoeness recorded the only miss, blazing over, before Anton Panenka made a name for himself. German keeper Sepp Maier, facing the decisive kick, dived slightly early – but Panenka cheekily chipped him for a famous victory.

In 1980, the quarter-finals were abolished and replaced by two groups of four. Belgium stunned England, Spain and hosts Italy to reach the semi-finals. Sadly, England's hooligan fans left their mark on the event, with riots marring the 1-1 draw with Belgium in Turin, where only 7,000 watched the match. The team won just once, against Spain, with goals by Trevor Brooking and Tony Woodcock, before departing for home.

Belgium, inspired by Wilfrid van Moer in midfield and the finishing skills of Jan Ceulemans, reached the final in Rome.

But they were no match for the Germans, who became the first country to win the trophy twice. Horst Hrubesch scored his second of the game in the final minutes for a 2-1 victory.

The French were unstoppable on home soil in 1984. A record nine goals in five games by midfield genius Michel Platini were just reward for a side that threw caution to the wind. Alongside Platini, elegant midfielders Alain Giresse, Jean Tigana and Luis Fernandez had all the answers – certainly more than Spain in the final, which the French won in Paris, 2-0.

A goal by European Footballer of the Year Allan Simonsen had given 10-1 outsiders Denmark a decisive 1-0 win at Wembley to put paid to England's chances of reaching the finals that year.

Holland's success in 1988 was as welcome for football as that of the French. Beaten twice in World Cup finals, the Dutch at last secured the major title their skills had so often deserved. They had impressed in a come-from-behind warm-up draw at Wembley just weeks before the finals. While this was not the total football side of Cruyff, Rep and Rensenbrink, they were packed with flair. The side was built around Ruud Gullit, Frank Rijkaard and striker Marco van Basten, whose career was later tragically cut short by a serious knee injury.

DUTCH MASTER: Ruud Gullit leads Holland to victory in 1988.

EURO History

TURNIPS 1'

The Republic of Ireland, managed by 1966 World Cup hero Jack Charlton, qualified for the finals – only to be drawn against England. BBC TV pundit Mark Lawrenson had scored a rare international goal in a qualifying-round win in Scotland, but the Irish surpassed themselves in Stuttgart as Ray Houghton's goal humbled Bobby Robson's England.

A hat-trick by van Basten in the next tie sealed England's fate, though the Russians, who beat the Dutch 1-0 thanks to Vassiliy Rats in their opener, won the group.

West Germany faced Holland in the semi-finals having not lost to them in 32 years. Jurgen Klinsmann went down under a slight challenge from Rijkaard and Lothar Matthaus scored from the spot to put the Germans ahead. But Gullit inspired the Dutch fight-back. Ronald Koeman and van Basten scored to book a rematch with the Russians in the final.

Holland took a 2-0 lead through Gullit and van Basten, and keeper Hans van Breukelen saved a penalty from Belanov before the outstanding Rijkaard wrapped up a comfortable victory.

Scotland made their finals debut in Sweden in 1992. But the surprise packet was to be Denmark. They had failed to qualify but were called up as a late replacement for war-ravaged Yugoslavia. The Danes had little time to prepare but, remarkably, went home with the trophy.

England, under Graham Taylor, were poor, failing to beat – or score against – Denmark and France after qualifying uneasily at the expense of the Republic of Ireland. They needed to beat the hosts in their final group game to reach the semi-finals and had the perfect start with a David Platt goal after three minutes. But Sweden equalised. Taylor panicked, taking off his most potent striker, skipper Gary Lineker, and Tomas Brolin, later to play for Leeds United, grabbed an 82nd-minute winner. It sparked the classic headline in *The Sun*: SWEDES 2 TURNIPS 1.

Scotland were far from outclassed when losing their opener 1-0 to Holland. Richard Gough was heroic in defence, keeping Gullit quiet, but a Dennis Bergkamp goal won it.

Drawn in the toughest section, the Scots then lost 2-0 to Germany, with Karlheinz Riedle and Steffen Effenberg scoring despite fierce Scots' pressure. They at least had some consolation from beating the CIS (formerly Soviet Union) 3-0 with goals by Paul McStay, Ally McCoist and a Gary McAllister penalty.

Holland were favourites to retain their crown but ran into a Danish side brimming with confidence. Brian Laudrup scored once as the match went to penalties. Van Basten had his kick saved by Peter Schmeichel but none of the Danes missed as the side reversed its fortune from four years earlier when losing a semi-final shoot-out to Spain.

Germany overcame the Swedes in the other semi-final but they fell behind after 18 minutes against Denmark when John Jensen drove home a rare goal (as Arsenal fans will testify from his time at Highbury!).

Schmeichel denied Klinsmann with an acrobatic save before the Danes added a decisive second, through Kim Vilfort, who scored after appearing to handle the ball.

Then came 1996 and all that, when the European Championships came to England, and England so nearly sent all the way.

Can Keegan's men go one better in the year 2000?

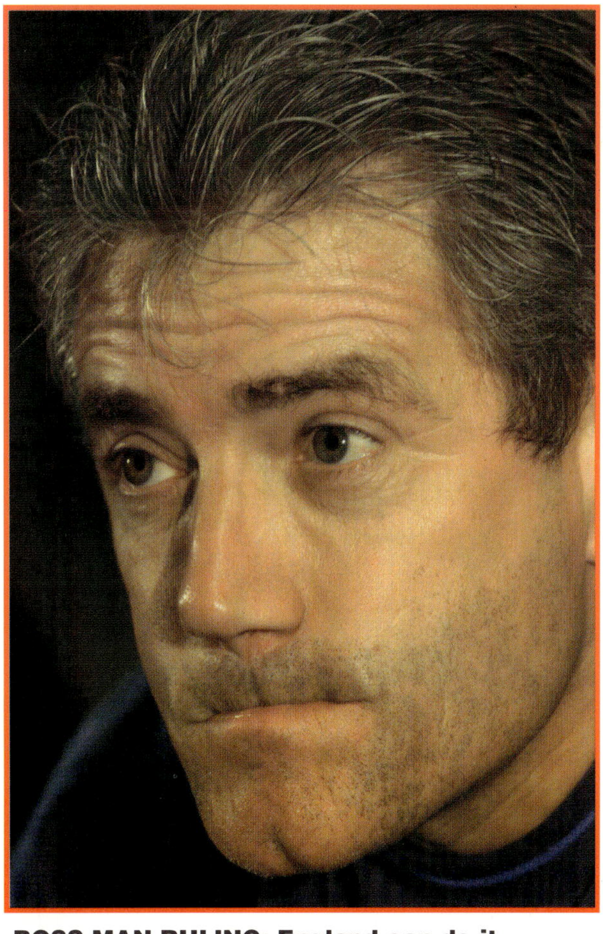

BOSS MAN RULING: England can do it, believes Keegan.

ENGLAND TAKE THE

GOLDEN SCHOLES: Paul gets a hug from Shearer after scoring against Scotland.

"AT LEAST WE'RE THERE!" Kevin Keegan's relief as England staggered over the line to reach the Euro2000 finals in Belgium and Holland this summer was shared by all the fans.

In the end they had to take the High Road to the Low Countries, qualifying via a two-leg play-off against old rivals Scotland after snatching second place in group five on goal difference.

The play-off was effectively settled in the first leg in Glasgow, where two goals from Paul Scholes gave England the kind of cushion that even a 1-0 defeat in the return at Wembley four days later could not dent.

However, England coach Keegan is well aware that a big improvement is essential if England are to make any real impact in the finals.

The harsh reality is that in ten matches so far in the competition England have managed just four victories, including two against tiny Luxembourg. And that, as Keegan knows, simply won't do.

England's campaign began in Sweden back in 1998 with a different coach, Glenn Hoddle in charge. But despite the boost of a first minute goal from skipper Alan Shearer, they succumbed to strikes from Andreas Andersson and Johan Mjallby. A 2-1 defeat was a terrible start, made even worse by the sending off of Paul Ince.

By the time England played again – a disappointing 0-0 draw with Bulgaria at Wembley - Sweden had claimed another victory, this time away in Bulgaria, and were already firm favourites to win the group.

Next stop Luxembourg, who were duly dispatched 3-0, thanks to goals from Michael Owen, Shearer and Gareth Southgate...then it was all change at the top. OUT went Hoddle and, after some delay, IN came the people's choice, Kevin Keegan – just in time to pick a squad for the crucial home game with Poland.

Three goals from Manchester United's Paul Scholes was enough to put the Euro campaign back on track, albeit briefly.
Jerzy Brzeczek grabbed the Polish goal. Keegan beamed as the nation roared its admiration, but not for long.

Group leaders Sweden, controlled and organised left Wembley with a deserved goal-less draw, putting automatic qualification almost out of England's reach.

England need maximum points from the final three games. In Bulgaria they grabbed an early lead

THAT'S MY BOY: Scholes again, this time with coach Kevin Keegan.

HIGH ROAD TO THE LOW COUNTRIES...

through Shearer, but three minutes later Gueorgui Markov equalised and, once again, England had to settle for a single point.

Thank heavens for Luxembourg. A six-nil scoreline at Wembley at least meant some entertainment for the fans. Three goals for Shearer this time, two from Steve Mcmanaman and a late strike from Michael Owen.

And so to the final group game in Poland, with a win guaranteeing second spot for England and a place in the play-offs. Once again, though, England found no way through a packed defence. The game finished without a goal, and England's fate was no longer in their own hands.

Now that vital second place relied on Sweden, who had already qualified, beating Poland in their final group game.

We watched, we waited, we cheered as first Kennet Andresson, then Celtic-based striker Henrik Larsson scored the second half goals that put Poland out..and sent England through to the play-offs with Scotland.

The Scots had finished as comfortable runners-up behind the Czechs in Group Nine. And they proved more than a match for England over the two legs in every department...except scoring goals.

It was that man Paul Scholes again who showed them the way with a brilliant double strike at Hampden Park to give England a 2-0 lead a the half-way stage. The spirited Scots took the Wembley return 1-0 thanks to a goal from Don Hutchinson, but Keegan's men held on.

The aggregate score was 2-1. We were there....

* Results and tables: Pages 174 and 175.

WHO LOST THEIR SHIRT ON SCOTLAND? Owen, Redknapp and Ince celebrate after England claim a place in the finals at the expense of the Scots.

TONY ADAMS

DEFENDER

Tony Adams has been the rock at the centre of England's defence for more than a decade. Young Guns have come and gone – all failing to dislodge the best domestic centre-back of his generation. Young Gunners, too, have failed to shift him at Highbury, where Adams is a living Arsenal legend, having won virtually all at club level.

Even during Arsenal's disappointing Champions' League ventures in recent seasons, which have seen their early exit, Adams has proved himself a giant.

But age is catching up with him and each season the papers trot out the story of how Adams is unlikely to carry his aching bones through the gruelling slog of another season. Each time, of course, he proves them wrong and eats up pre-season training, ready for the campaign ahead. He just loves football and can't imagine his life without a game that has saved him from self-destruction.

Adams undoubtedly has his club boss Arsene Wenger to thank for lengthening his career. The Frenchman has backed Adams through personal crises and worked hard on the player's fitness and diet. He has nursed him through difficult times when the physical pain – mostly from his back – has become too much, often sending him for rest and treatment in the sun.

Adams then returns, fired up and fresh for the important business in hand. His fitness after a long season with his club is the sole shadow hanging over Adams' ability to be in the vanguard for England. And Adams will take what rest is offered and devote himself to the cause.

"Playing for England is a different challenge altogether. I love pulling on that white shirt. It makes me feel so proud," says Adams.

And putting on the captain's armband, as he did regularly when he played under Terry Venables, was a source of even greater pride. Glenn Hoddle later stripped Adams of the captaincy, handing it instead to Alan Shearer. Kevin Keegan succeeded Hoddle but left the dressing-room pecking-order untouched.

Some insiders claim it led to a rift between Adams and Shearer, though the Arsenal man diplomatically refuses to talk about it, save to say that he was very disappointed not to be leading his country. Adams is someone who loves to lead by example. He rolls up his sleeves and gets stuck in. It takes more than a few stitches before he will come off the field, whether he is playing for club or country.

He is a huge admirer of his Gunners team-mate Martin Keown, whom he says doesn't get the praise he deserves. He gets a sense of security with Keown beside him for England and David Seaman behind him in goal. But he's also a big fan of Sol Campbell – though he has to whisper his kind words for a Spurs man!

"We've got the players to do the job whatever the formation the boss chooses. And there are some good young players, like Jonathon Woodgate and Rio Ferdinand, coming through and I'm sure their time will come," says Adams.

Not too soon, though, he says! "I love winning. I've won a lot with Arsenal and now I'd love to win a big one with England."

Euro2000 verdict: Adams could yet be the apple of Keegan's eye.

STATS

Born: 10 October, 1966, Romford.

Club: Arsenal.

Fee: None, Arsenal junior.

QUOTE

'I love pulling on that white shirt. It makes me proud.'

DID YOU KNOW?

He's the most successful Arsenal captain in the club's history.

ENGLAND
5

NICOLAS ANELKA

STRIKER

Controversy seems destined to follow Nicolas Anelka until the day he retires. The young Frenchman seemed to have the world at his feet when he took England apart in a friendly for the World champions at Wembley. That after winning the Premiership and FA Cup Double with Arsenal. But his stay at Highbury, after Arsene Wenger had shrewdly 'stolen' him away from Paris St Germain, was always uneasy. There were reports of Anelka being homesick; of not liking the English lifestyle. Even rows about team-mates refusing to pass to him.

It was the long-running saga of his departure from the Gunners – eventually to Real Madrid for a staggering £23m – that left him with the tag as one of the most hated players in Europe. To even loyal Gunners fans he was Le Brat.

To be fair, though, much was down to the influence of his brothers, who act as his agents. When he was ordered to attend a function hosted by Spain's Prime Minister for his French opposite number – without his brothers – Anelka sulked. Eventually he relented, but it put his tenure at the club he supposedly idolised, in major jeopardy.

By the time France completed their uneasy passage to Euro2000 last October, Anelka was still looking for his first goal for Real and pleading with fans to be patient. He finally broke his duck in January's FIFA Club World Championships in Brazil. But his missed penalty cost Real a place in the final, and he picked up a major knee injury that meant a long lay-off.

Real president Lorenzo Sanz described his signing of Anelka as 'a beautiful madness'. To all but Arsenal, who profited massively in the end, it was just, simply, mad.

Anelka's own sanity was tested, though, by his poor form. "People don't seem to realise how hard it has been for me to come to a new club and a new country," he said after one embarrassing Real defeat. "Everything is different. The football is slower than in England, where it was about chasing long balls. Sometimes it feels like I'm not getting any service at all."

Arsenal fans will remember such comments, aimed at Dutch pair Marc Overmars and Dennis Bergkamp. "I understand that people are impatient with me," said Anelka. "But things will get better with time. I remember people saying the same things at Arsenal and I answered the critics with a lot of goals once I settled into the team."

The youngster's international career has suffered, too. He was substituted after 55 minutes of France's Euro2000 qualifier in the Ukraine, a 0-0 draw. Then he was ignored for the last two matches of the campaign, in Armenia and against Iceland at the Stade de Paris.

At one point, after returning to Madrid from international duty, he told the media: "I just want a quiet life and I can't get it here. And if I can't enjoy football, maybe it's better to give up." His brothers denied he said it; his fellow professionals, like team-mate Roberto Carlos, doubted that he meant it.

There is no doubt that France needs a striker of Anelka's talents to finish the work of their wonderfully gifted midfield. However, this much-troubled youngster will need to have got his head straight first if he is to answer his country's call this summer.

Euro2000 verdict: Will the real Anelka please stand up...

STATS

Born: 14 March, 1979, Paris.

Club: Real Madrid.

Fee: £23m from Arsenal, 1999.

QUOTE

'Signing Anelka's a beautiful madness.'

REAL CHIEF LORENZO SANZ

DID YOU KNOW?

Nic had to wait six months for his first Real goal.

adidas
17

MARKUS BABBEL
DEFENDER

Markus Babbel has his eyes set on twin targets this summer. The Bayern Munich defender wants to see Germany retain the European championship – before he completes a dream move to Liverpool.

"I want to try something new," he says. "Liverpool is a traditional club with a high profile. They appeal to me very much.

"Bayern made me a very generous offer to stay but the way things are looking, I'll be leaving this summer. Liverpool look the ideal club for me." He recently signed a pre-contract agreement with the Anfield club.

The 27-year-old defender says he has still not recovered from the last-gasp Champions' Cup final defeat against Manchester United. He wanted an early chance to get back at the Old Trafford club who made him a transfer target several years ago but could not agree personal terms.

United wanted to sign him after playing a starring role in Germany's Euro96 success. He recalls: "The clubs had agreed on a fee of around £5m but then they said: "No – we don't want you any more".

"I was devastated because it was a dream for me to play for them."

He believes he was treated badly by United, who said his wage demands were too high.

"It was not true. They said I was money-grabbing and I got a very bad reputation, which I did not deserve.

"In the end I believe they just used me to try to get another player. I found out later they really wanted Miguel Nadal of Barcelona – but they didn't buy him either."

There would have been a small irony had he joined Sir Alex Ferguson's side – Babbel reveals that Manchester City were the first club he supported as a boy. "I loved to watch English football on television and I just took to following City," he says.

The father of two stalled a move to Anfield a year ago because he wanted to see if Bayern could make amends for their European final defeat.

He has won almost 50 international caps and is in his second spell with Bayern. The German champions were keen to keep the commanding central defender, but club president Franz Beckenbauer says: "Markus has said that he will definitely be going to Liverpool."

He looks forward to Germany's clash with England and says: "We are good enough to beat anyone, including England, and we can successfully defend our title.

"The match against England is a footballing classic and I'm sure it'll be a great contest.

"If we play to our potential, I don't think we've got anything to worry about. I'm confident we can get through, although we must not underestimate Romania or Portugal."

Euro2000 verdict: Tower of Babbel vital to Germany's chances

STATS

Born: 8 September, 1972, Munich.

Club: Bayern Munich.

Previous club: Hamburg, left July 1994.

QUOTE

"The match with England will be a classic."

DID YOU KNOW?

He used to support Manchester City as a boy.

adidas
4

DAVID BECKHAM
MIDFIELDER

Kevin Keegan reckons David Beckham has what it takes to become one of the game's golden greats. And this summer's big European tournament provides the young star, narrowly beaten by Rivaldo for the World Footballer of the Year accolade following his treble-winning year of glory with Manchester United, with the perfect platform to display his remarkable talents.

1999 was topped off with United's fantastic Champions Cup final victory over Bayern Munich. Can 2000 bring even greater glory? The England coach says: "Everyone remembers David's World Cup sending off – and the one for United in Brazil this year – and I know he wants to do all he can to make amends.

"I always say to the strikers that if you win four free-kicks around the box, David will score from one. If you get him three, he'll probably score one. Even if you get only two, there's a decent chance he'll still score. He's a real talent and yet he's not the finished article yet, for all that he's won in the game."

Keegan says Beckham is an asset even in his quieter games. "Teams overload their formation to try to subdue him and cut out his tremendously accurate crosses. That creates holes for others, like Paul Scholes, to exploit.

"I've seen it with United many times. Now I have seen it first-hand with England. He can go on to win it all before he finishes in the game."

Beckham was hurt by the reaction to his moment of red-card madness against Argentina. Fans and media blamed him for killing off England's World Cup hopes in France. He says: "I think the majority of people still dislike me, but maybe they respect me a bit more after winning the treble with United."

Beckham fears he will never be allowed to forget his clash with Diego Simeone, right under the ref's nose, that made him the subject of so much open hatred. "I accept that I'll have to deal with it for the rest of my career. The stigma will stay with me," he says.

"It's sad to see kids of six or seven, sitting with their dads as they abuse me. What chance have the kids got with parents like that?"

Beckham speaks with some authority as a dad himself to baby Brooklyn, and husband to Spice Girl Victoria Adams. He's a happy man right now – and who could argue? Yet he still has so much ambition.

"Even being mentioned as a contender for world's best foootballer was incredible for me. It was the ultimate, a dream come true. To be mentioned alongside the likes of Pele, Ronaldo and Zidane is such an honour.

"But I still have so much to learn. My tackling could do with some improvement. Maybe I have to calm down a little – but my fiery attitude is never going away completely," Beckham says. Will distractions away from football affect his motivation, having achieved so much at such a young age? Beckham is positive that his pop-star lifestyle, criticised by United boss Sir Alex Ferguson, can be controlled.

"People get the impression that I spend my time going from fashion shows to parties and so on. But it is not like that at all. Football – and family – come first," he says. Although David Beckham has long since abandoned all hope of a normal life. "I never complain about the fame, though I never set out looking for it," he says.

Euro2000 verdict: The bottle of Becks is about to be tested to the full.

STATS

Born: 2 May, 1975, Leytonstone.

Club: Manchester United.

Fee: None. United juniors.

QUOTE

"He can win it all before he retires."

KEVIN KEEGAN

DID YOU KNOW?

He was 'discovered' in a Bobby Charlton soccer school.

UMBRO
7
UMBRO

HENNING BERG

DEFENDER

Henning Berg had been a transfer target for ten years before Alex Ferguson was able to sign him from Blackburn Rovers for £5m in August 1997. That's how highly the Manchester United manager rates the Norwegian central defender.

Rovers made £4.6m on the deal, having lured him from Lillestrom for just £400,000 in January 1993. But Sir Alex believes he got the better end of the deal. Berg is solid, reliable, and looks calm and assured at the back for club and country. Berg has won almost 70 international caps and now a growing number of honours with United, including Premiership titles in 1995 and 1999.

United tried to bring him to Old Trafford when he was 17 but could not secure a work permit. Kenny Dalglish succeeded, much to Ferguson's disappointment. Berg impressed with his adjustment to life in the Premiership while he was at Ewood. Coincidentally, he was sent off for the first time in his career for a controversial foul on Lee Sharpe in a 4-2 defeat by United.

Permit problems later squared the circle for Berg. United failed in an attempt to sign Brazilian Celio Silva, so Fergie called for Berg to plug his defensive problems. The move made him the most expensive defender in the Premiership. That fee is less than half the £10.5m United paid for Jaap Stam, but Berg is certainly not half the player.

He briefly lost out to Gary Pallister and Ronny Johnsen and threatened to leave United unless he got a regular place in the side. Berg feared he might lose his place in Norway's World Cup squad. But the rift was healed and, after recovering from a series of injuries, Berg went on to prove his worth for the Reds alongside Stam despite further pressure from the arrival of young Frenchman Mikael Silvestre.

Berg was at his best in the Champions' League quarter-final against Inter Milan in 1999. He made a superb telling goal-line clearance at Old Trafford to keep the tie alive and deny the Italians an away goal. At the San Siro a fortnight later, he kept Ronaldo shackled brilliantly.

He has featured regularly in Norway's run to the Euro200 finals. They conceded only nine goals in their ten qualifying matches – three of those in their opening defeat by Latvia, the one blemish on an otherwise impressive record.

Berg believes that they can come through their opening group, with seeded Spain, Yugoslavia and Slovenia and will be dangerous opponents. They have already beaten the Slovenes twice – 4-0 and 2-1.

"But we are taking nothing for granted. It is an open tournament and we have enough talent in the squad to be confident of our chances," he says.

He played a starring role for Norway in the World Cup, as Norway beat Brazil 2-1 in their group clash. Losing to Italy 1-0 in the second round was a bitter disappointment. But he says: "I think we have learned a lot from that result and we have a number of talented younger players who have come through since then. It will be exciting this summer."

Euro2000 verdict: A number of forwards will founder on this Ice Berg...

STATS

Born: 1 September, 1969, Eidsvell, Norway.

Club: Manchester United.

Fee: £5m from Blackburn Rovers, August 1997.

QUOTE

"It is an open tournament - we can win it."

DID YOU KNOW?

Alex Ferguson waited 10 years to sign Henning.

UMBRO
FIFA WORLD CUP
FRANCE 1998
4

PATRIK BERGER

MIDFIELDER

The Czechs had the perfect run to Euro2000, not dropping a single point in qualifying. And they have never finished lower than third when reaching the European Championship finals.

But, says Patrik Berger, after their defeat by Germany in the Euro96 final, anything less than victory this time will be a disappointment.

Berger shot to prominence in Euro96. Little could he know, however, when he played for the Czechs at Anfield, that it would soon be his new football home. The Reds moved in shortly after the finals to complete a dream transfer for Berger, who, as a youngster in his native land, dreamed of Liverpool and idolised Kenny Dalglish.

"I had all sorts of memorabilia, collected for me by friends. I'd borrow and trade stuff all the time," Berger recalls. "I used to prize stuff collected from Liverpool's big European matches – programmes, tickets and such. Then to find myself playing for Liverpool was amazing."

He has fond memories from playing for his country, too. Berger impressed with his pace and close control in Euro96 and says the squad were a little surprised to have done as well as they did in reaching the final.

"I think a lot of us would have settled for qualifying from the opening group. But once we got to the knockout stages we thought: why can't we go all the way here?"

Now, though, the Czechs are the second top-rated side in the world, something that astonishes the modest Berger. He of course scored for the Czechs in the Euro96 final, when they were beaten by Oliver Bierhoff's golden goal in extra-time – the first to settle a major final. "That was very scary, knowing that any slip could cost you the final. The Germans are always very tough to beat – they never give up until the final whistle."

Berger will actually miss the first two matches in the Euro2000 finals after being sent off in the last qualifying match, against the Faroe Islands. The Liverpool midfielder faced a very nervous run-up to the finals to see whether he would be omitted from coach Josef Chovanec's squad. After all, it might be viewed as a luxury having a player eligible for just one of the opening group games. And his team-mate in 1996, defender Tomas Repka, was left out from the squad after being similarly red-carded.

However, it seems difficult to believe that the Czechs will leave behind the left-footed Berger, whose former clubs include Slavia Prague and Borussia Dortmund.

Berger says Euro96 did so much for him and tips a colleague, Jan Koller, to be the big breakthrough name of Euro2000. Koller, who scored six goals in qualifying and had a run of nine in ten games, has come from nowhere to be the new national hero. He plays his football for Anderlecht, in Belgium, but was playing in fourth division football back home when he was discovered. "Jan has a great future ahead of him. He has a real eye for goal and that has made us a better team than in 1996," says Berger.

Euro2000 verdict: Czechs will rely on Berger King to provide the killer passes.

STATS

Born: 10 November, 1973, Prague, Czech Republic.

Club: Liverpool.

Fee: £3.25m from Borussia Dortmund, August 1996.

QUOTE

"The golden goal is such a scary way to finish games."

DID YOU KNOW?

He's suspended for the first two games in Euro2000.

puma
14
14
Fair Play
puma

DENNIS BERGKAMP

STRIKER

Euro2000 may be Dennis Bergkamp's farewell to international football. It's not that he's past it. Indeed, the dynamic Dutchman is not yet 31. But with the next World Cup in Japan and South Korea in two years' time and Bergkamp terrified of flying, he is unlikely to be available for the national team then.

Fortunately for the Arsenal striker, this summer's big soccerfest is partly on home soil. And the matches in nearby Belgium will be a bus-ride away at most.

Bergkamp is keen to sign off with a major trophy at international level to go with his domestic awards from his time in Holland, Italy and England. And he is especially anxious to erase the memory of Holland's 4-1 mauling by England in Euro96. "I was surprised at our own performance, just falling apart like that. Normally our defence is our strength but we made so many errors," he remembers.

Dennis the Menace did at least leave his mark on the World Cup, when Holland finished a more glorious fourth. He scored a simply sublime goal to beat England's conquerors, Argentina. Taking a long ball from deep on his instep, he tamed its pace, switched feet and delivered a killing blow with the coolness of a trained assassin.

It left his Arsenal manager, Arsene Wenger, drooling at his good fortune. For Wenger arrived at Highbury from Japan to inherit Bergkamp, a club record £7.5m buy from Inter Milan. Wenger was not alone in the Bergkamp fan club, though.

Former Ajax manager Louis van Gaal, and the great Johan Cruyff, have worked with Bergkamp and admired his skillls from his youngest days. Indeed, Cruyff was coach when Bergkamp broke into the Ajax first team at 17. "They didn't think I'd make it for a time, because I was so lightweight. But Cruyff encouraged me, along with the other promising younger players. Many of them are now in the national team, of course."

Bergkamp has changed over the years, asserting himself in a more physical fashion, particularly since joining Arsenal. Van Gaal says: "Dennis always needed to put his authority on the game more. He is an intelligent player who is finally beginning to fulfil his potential."

Despite lucrative offers from Spain in particular, Bergkamp committed himself to finish his playing days at Arsenal, where he is idolised almost as much as in Holland. He returns to the Netherlands regularly and retains a great sense of belonging to his homeland and his family. Bergkamp still recalls his early days when "my first contract at Ajax earned me more in one year than my father ever made. It put things into perspective and I have never forgotten that".

And the fans won't forget Bergkamp. Gunners supporters will recall the Premiership and FA Cup double of a couple of years ago. Dutch fans will forever remember his World Cup quarter-final special. They would love to remember him for something else, too – a return to the glories of 1988 when, captained by Ruud Gullit, the Orange last lifted the European Championship trophy.

Euro2000 verdict: It could be a bus-ride to glory for this Premiership legend.

STATS

Born: 18 May, 1969, Amsterdam.

Club: Arsenal.

Fee: £7.5m from Inter Milan, 1995.

QUOTE

' I was so light they didn't think I'd make a footballer. '

DID YOU KNOW?

He was named Dennis after Scottish legend Denis Law.

10

OLIVER BIERHOFF

STRIKER

When it comes to belting out the national anthem before the big matches, or in a triumphant bath afterwards, Oliver Bierhoff is the man who often hits all the right notes. And, when you watch the two-goal hero of Germany's Euro96 success on the football field – all Teutonic muscle and power – you can't imagine him dressed in a white gown and ruff, singing hymns. But that is what he used to do in his early teen years. He was a choirboy.

The AC Milan striker says: "Yes, it is true that I used to sing in a choir. But my voice has changed a bit since then!"

He wasn't singing a terribly happy tune last season in Milan, who were bundled out of both the Champions' League and the UEFA Cup in short order. They averaged just a goal a game in the Champions' League, in Chelsea's opening group. Bierhoff at least was on target against the Blues in the San Siro in a 1-1 draw. Their defeat by Galatasaray sent them to the bottom of their section and cost them a shot at the UEFA Cup.

Yet with Bierhoff, George Weah and Ukraine star Andrei Schevchenko in the ranks, the then Italian champions should have had more to offer. International duties gave Bierhoff a bit more to sing about last season. The man whose two goals in the Euro96 final secured the title for Germany, was a major part of their Group 3 success, albeit narrowly from the dangerous Turks, who had won the first encounter 1-0 in Bursa.

Bierhoff struck both goals in a crucial 2-1 success in Finland in September and was on target again four days later as the Germans overwhelmed Northern Ireland 4-0 in Dortmund. He scored a hat-trick in the 6-1 qualifying win over Moldova and scored another goal in a 3-1 win against the same side in Chisinau.

"I love the feeling of playing for my country," says Bierhoff. "And I have very fond memories of the last European Championship, particularly the final. I had been on the fringe of things, always on the bench, and it seemed I would not get my chance. Eventually I did and it was fantastic to score the winning goals, especially at Wembley.

"Wembley has a special place in football and Germany have enjoyed good and bad moments there. In some ways it was disappointing not to be playing England in the final itself."

He said German teams have a certain mind-set that refuses to allow them to give in. "We are winners and have this mentality – all German teams have it and that is why we have done so well in major competitions.

"The last World Cup was a rare failure for us. The 3-0 defeat against Croatia in the quarter-finals was a real shock. It took a long time for it to sink in. The warnings had been there – we were losing to Yugoslavia and Mexico but got results. Perhaps we had too many older players in the team."

Bierhoff is now one of the elder statesmen of the side, at 32, and indeed its captain. He has enjoyed moderate success at club level and it was his Euro96 exploits that won him a move to Udinese in Italy.

Jurgen Klinsmann cast a long shadow in the national team and it was Euro96 that allowed him to emerge as a power in his own right. He was surprised that no major Premiership club tried to lure him to England. "I think my style of play would be well suited," he says. He may have to settle for crossing swords again with England in Euro2000 – and again in qualifying for the next World Cup. "That's one I'm looking forward to – we always raise our game for matches against England."

Euro2000 verdict: Biers all round if Oliver's army retain their title.

STATS

Born: 1 May, 1968, Karlsruhe.

Club: AC Milan.

Previous club: Valencia, July 1998.

QUOTE

"It was fantastic to score the winner at Wembley."

DID YOU KNOW?

Germany's captain used to be a choirboy at school.

adidas
9

GIANLUIGI BUFFON

GOALKEEPER

Gianluigi Buffon has it tough when it comes to pulling on the keeper's shirt for his country. His forwards may miss an open goal, the midfielders may misplace a pass. And the men in front of him might make a mess of an attempted clearance. But there are no second chances for Buffon.

It's not simply the case that he's the last line of defence. More that his coach, Dino Zoff, is watching every move he makes. And no-one knows the goalkeeper's art quite like Zoff.

For he is the man who collected football's greatest prize, the World Cup, in 1982, as Italy's captain. It was Zoff who was still an established international goalkeeper at the ripe old age of 40, before going into coaching.

But Buffon is no buffoon. The young Parma goalkeeper, who has seen off the challenges of Angelo Peruzzi and Gianluca Pagliuca, believes that having the maestro in charge is a help, not a handicap.

At 21, Buffon has what it takes to be Italy's first-choice keeper for more than a decade ahead. And he has the maturity to know that he doesn't know it all. Who better to have by your side as your mentor, pointing out your faults, the areas to work on and improve, and to encourage your strengths, than Zoff?

Buffon is an extremely confident young man. Parma have the reputation for being one of the more attack-minded clubs in Serie A. But the shrewd judges have long noted Buffon's contribution to their recent successes. Indeed, it could be argued that his talents have helped them to become genuine title contenders at last.

The most remarkable thing about Buffon is that he has been given his chance at such a tender age, particularly in the world's toughest domestic league. He made his first-team debut while still a teenager – a rarity in itself. And he was elevated to the senior international team while still eligible for the Under-21s – not so rare for outfield players, but very much so for keepers. That shows how much confidence Zoff has in him. Buffon came in for the Euro2000 qualifier against Switzerland, keeping a clean sheet in the 2-0 win in Udine. He missed the next couple of games, both friendlies, but was back between the posts for the crucial 2-1 win against Denmark in Copenhagen. He then shut out the opposition in three of the next four games.

Zoff kept faith with the youngster, even after Italy squandered a 2-0 lead to suffer a shock 3-2 home defeat against the Danes – and he responded superbly as Italy battled to the goal-less draw in Belarus that secured their automatic qualification place, ahead of Denmark.

Buffon is a superbly agile player who, unlike the traditional Italian keeper, looks happy when collecting crosses. And he has already collected a European trophy – the 1999 UEFA Cup with Parma, in a year that saw his club qualify for the Champions' League.

Now he is about to move up a gear in his quest for honours at international level, with Zoff's praise ringing in his ears.

"Gigi is a very competent goalkeeper and shows a maturity that is surprising for one so young," says the coach. "He makes me wish I was his age again! He can achieve so much in the game."

Euro2000 verdict: Watch for this star of the next decade.

STATS

Born: 28 January, 1978, Parma.

Club: Parma.

Fee: None. Parma junior.

QUOTE

"He makes me wish I was his age again. He can achieve so much."

DINO ZOFF

DID YOU KNOW?

Gigi has already won a European trophy - the UEFA Cup, with Parma.

12
reusch
reusch

SOL CAMPBELL

DEFENDER

Sol Campbell is one of the hottest properties in the English game. And he's an Englishman. That's rare these days, with so many foreign stars invading the Premiership. The Tottenham Hotspur defender is keeping the London club on tenterhooks over whether he'll stay with them when his contract expires next summer. And there will be no shortage of takers if George Graham can't find the cash to keep the Sol Man at White Hart Lane.

Manchester United and the rest of Europe's elite will be knocking at his door. For Campbell is a real talent. He is athletic, reads the game well and possesses a great deal of natural skill. The sight of Campbell striding forward from central defence, taking on all-comers, as he did in that memorable World Cup clash with Argentina a couple of years ago, was stirring for all England fans. It is rare to see an English defender risk all in such dashing fashion – and have the skill to carry it off.

Indeed, many fans wish he was given rein to do more of that sort of raiding, particularly with England's lack of midfield vision and incisiveness. Once Campbell gets in full stride, he is a very hard man to stop. The only sad thing is that he often takes one touch too many and loses control when he has won a great position to get in a strike.

Not that he's shot-shy, as he has proved for Tottenham, often scoring crucial goals for his club. Indeed he thought he had scored against Argentina, only for his towering header to be ruled out by a foul by Alan Shearer elsewhere in the six-yard box. It would have been no less than Campbell deserved. He was a rock for England that day, especially after they lost David Beckham to a red card.

Kevin Keegan thinks the world of Campbell, but injury has all too often restricted the player's selection since the England coach succeeded Glenn Hoddle during England's Euro2000 qualifying campaign. Campbell would be one of the first names pencilled in by Keegan.

He says: "Sol is a superb player. Any manager would love to have him in their team. He defends well. He never commits himself and makes the defender make the mistake.

"He is a model for any youngster to study. He stays on his feet, presents a huge barrier and you seldom see him beaten for speed as he's such a great athlete.

"But there is a lot more to Sol's game. He is so versatile. You can play him at full-back, as we did in our play-off win against Scotland at Hampden Park, or central defence. You can even throw him forward in the dying moments if you are desperate for a goal.

"He's strong in the air and formidable on the deck. A superb player."

Campbell came through the junior ranks at Tottenham and it would be a huge blow for them if he leaves. But he has ambitions to win things – the Coca-Cola Cup success against Leicester in 1999 is his only major medal to date, and it would be no surprise if Spurs raked in a world-record fee for a defender rather than let him go for free when his contract ends.

"When it comes to playing for England, I'll be putting all thoughts about my future to one side," he says. "I want success, and there's no reason why we can't do really well this summer."

Euro2000 verdict: Heart and Sol – that's Campbell.

STATS

Born: 18 September, 1974, Newham, London.

Club: Tottenham Hotspur.

Fee: None. Tottenham juniors.

QUOTE

"He's a model for any youngster to study."

KEVIN KEEGAN

DID YOU KNOW?

He was christened Sulzeer Jeremiah Campbell.

6

FABIO CANNAVARO

DEFENDER

They say the most talented players often learn their craft at the knee of legends. That is especially true of Fabio Cannavaro, one of Italy's most accomplished and stylish defenders.

At 11, he was a ball-boy in his native Naples. One day, into the lads' dressing-rooms strode Diego Maradona, Napoli's Argentine genius, then the best player in the world. Match time was beckoning, but a star-struck Cannavaro and his great idol had a brief kickabout that has since been ingrained in the current Parma star's memory.

"You can't imagine what it was like for me," says Cannavaro who, at 14, was snapped up by Napoli. They saw real potential in him – if not as the next Maradona.

"He juggled the ball as only he can. Then he passed it among us and watched us kicking it around, it was incredible – and that was only half of it." He found fame not at his home-town club, but at Parma, who bought him from a then-ailing Napoli in 1995. He had worked his way through to the Napoli first team to make his debut in a 4-3 defeat at Juventus.

A great student of the defender's art, Cannavaro learned much from watching such icons of Italian football as Franco Baresi, who retired a few years ago, and Paolo Maldini, the national captain.

"I watched Maradona try to get the better of Baresi but he never missed a tackle, for all the tricks Diego could find," recalls Cannavaro. "He was a rock."

And now, he says, it is a joy to play in the national side alongside Maldini. "He has such power and pace. I never imagined we would be in the same team."

It was Maldini's father, Cesare, who promoted Cannavaro from the Under-21s to the senior national team in 1997. His debut was against Northern Ireland and his second full start was against England at Wembley for the World Cup qualifier that Italy won with a Gianfranco Zola goal.

Cannavaro has been a key player for Parma in their recent rise to prominence, featuring in their UEFA Cup victories of 1995 and 1999. "It was a good move for me, even though I was sad to leave Napoli," he says. "The club was in a terrible mess when I left."

Now, having won honours for his club, he believes it is time to do the same in the blue of Italy. "With the talented players we have in the squad, we are capable of doing very well in the finals," he says.

"I think we are strong in all positions and people should not take too much notice of the way we played in the qualifying games. It is what happens in the summer that counts.

"For me, I would like it to be a stepping stone to success in the next World Cup. That's the biggest stage, one that made Maradona's name. But to be European champions along the way would be a tremendous achievement."

Euro2000 verdict: He can be absolutely Fab...

STATS

Born: 13 September, 1973, Naples.

Club: Parma.

Previous club: Napoli, signed 1995.

QUOTE

'Maradona was my absolute idol at Napoli.'

DID YOU KNOW?

He has won two UEFA Cups with Parma.

4
NIKE

RUI COSTA

MIDFIELDER

Rui Costa is something of a throwback to days when midfield generals strutted their stuff – when players like Michel Platini and Glenn Hoddle sprayed passes round, trying to unpick tight defences. Watching a talented playmaker at work is one of the most thrilling sights in football. Zinedine Zidane is the current heartbeat of the French side, and Rui Costa does the same for Portugal.

He is a tall, elegant player, with an upright stance that gives him visual command of the pitch. And he can deliver a killer pass – just ask his Fiorentina team-mate Gabriel Batistuta. The Argentinian hit-man has plundered the quality service supplied by Rui Costa to make him the most feared marksman in Serie A.

Sadly for Portuguese fans, Rui Costa – full name Rui Manuel Cesar Costa – has had to pursue the bulk of his career abroad. But the Lisbon-born midfielder did begin his career with Benfica, Portugal's most famous club. However, it was the fallen giants' perilous financial situation that led to him being sold to the Florence club in 1994 for £5m. That made him the costliest foreign import to Serie A that summer and kept Benfica afloat.

But Rui Costa's fortunes were followed closely by his army of fans back home. He had helped Benfica to success in the Portuguese league and cup in his three seasons at the Stadium of Light and there was a great deal of sadness at his departure.

In 1991, Rui Costa was a member of his country's World Under-20 championship-winning squad. The Portuguese were so impressed with the feat that they named their biggest club youth competition after him.

It was not long before he was elevated to the senior international side and he was the hub of their midfield in Euro96 in England.

Much was expected of Portugal and they were a big disappointment. This time round, expectations are again high. At 28, Rui Costa is still young enough to be involved with their World Cup campaign, although he might be past his best when the next European Championships come around, hosted by Portugal.

Rui Costa will be a central figure when the Portuguese tackle England in the teams' opening Group A clash in Eindhoven. He is optimistic of Portugal's chances, saying: "England are very inconsistent. One day they are good, the next they are bad. Hopefully we'll meet them on one of their bad days."

Everton's Abel Xavier says Rui Costa could be Portugal's trump card in the finals. "He is a very gifted player who creates chances for others but also scores many himself. He will be very important to the team."

Rui Costa believes it is time Portugal claimed a major prize after years of unfulfilled promise. "It is especially important for us as we stage the finals in 2004 – and it is vital to win the opening game against England," he says.

Euro2000 verdict: He would Costa fortune on the transfer market...

STATS

Born: 29 March, 1972, Lisbon.

Club: Fiorentina.

Fee: £5m from Benfica, July 1994.

QUOTE

"We must win our opening game against England."

DID YOU KNOW?

His £5m transfer to Italy kept Benfica afloat.

10

EDGAR DAVIDS

MIDFIELDER

While the likes of Ronaldo and Zinedine Zidane took centre stage in the last World Cup in France, those really in the know – the world's best coaches – had their own view of the best player in the tournament. And Edgar Davids was a name in most of the pundits' dream teams.

He is quite simply one of the best midfielders in the world. He is a rare blend of skill and tenacity. It is for his tough streak that his former coach at Ajax nicknamed Davids 'The Pitbull', after that ferocious breed of dog.

Davids, 27, lives up to his name at every opportunity and has a reputation for being in trouble both on and off the field.

His big sports hero is the NBA basketball icon Dennis Rodman, a one-time boyfriend of Madonna, and a man with a bad-boy reputation not unlike Davids.

Yet, away from football, Davids can be mild-mannered. He is widely read and said to be a keen student of Buddhist philosophy.

So much happened for Davids at a young age. He was born of Dutch Surinamese parents in Paramaribo, and was thrust into the Ajax first team while still a teenager, winning the Champions' League within the first three years.

He moved on a free transfer to AC Milan but it proved to be a disaster as he failed to fit into coach Fabio Capello's teams' plans and fell out with several of his colleagues. Davids was sold to arch-rivals Juventus, where he linked up with Dutch team-mates Patrick Kluivert, Clarence Seedorf, Michael Reiziger and Aron Winter, as well as becoming Zidane's favourite midfield partner.

With Juve he reached successive Champions' League finals, the last in 1998 when the Italian aces were beaten by Real Madrid – ironically in Amsterdam.

It was the Dutch contingent at the club that championed his return to the international side. He had disgraced himself at Euro96 by being sent home following a massive bust-up in the pre-tournament training camp in England.

Davids was one of the most vocal in putting his strong views as racial tensions in the Dutch camp boiled over into open warfare. He accused coach Guus Hiddink of favouring the white players in the squad over those from the Dutch West Indies or Surinam – and was promptly ordered to pack his bags. He missed the Dutch defeat by England at Wembley, when the lack of morale in the camp was obvious.

It said much of his return to peak form that Hiddink accepted Davids back into the fold for the World Cup, where his performances won comparisons with Johann Neeskens, the Dutch midfield master of the 1970s.

His tackling was as fierce as ever, despite the tougher refereeing, but Davids showed there was so much more to his game, with some shrewd passing. He has a fine football brain.

Hiddink, since succeeded by Frank Rijkaard, says: "I thought Edgar had an exceptional World Cup. He showed he has real talent and appeared to have matured at long last. He will be very important for the squad in the European finals."

Euro2000 verdict: 'The Pitbull' is straining at the leash...

STATS

Born: 13 March, 1973, Paramaribo, Surinam.

Club: Juventus.

Previous clubs: Ajax, AC Milan.

QUOTE

'He had an exceptional World Cup.'

GUUS HIDDINK

DID YOU KNOW?

Davids reads Buddhist philosophy in his spare time.

16

GILLES DE BILDE

STRIKER

Gilles De Bilde is known as 'The Beast' for his troublesome reputation on and off the field. Perhaps it is only right that, at international level, he plays for a team known as The Red Devils.

Last year saw a big turn-round in his career, with his £3m move to Sheffield Wednesday – where he immediately became a fans' favourite with his no-nonsense approach and eye for goal. He was also back in the fold for Belgium, after being something of an outcast following some violent episodes.

The double good news is that the Belgians' other major strike star of the past decade, Luc Nilis, has ended his self-imposed exile from international football and the former PSV Eindhoven duo could yet find themselves working in tandem again for their country in Euro2000.

Trouble seems to court De Bilde, who once received a suspended jail sentence and a big fine for two violent incidents, including one on the football field. He threw a punch that broke the eye socket of an opponent some years ago when he played for Anderlecht against Eendracht Aalst in the Belgian First Division. It was at Aalst that De Bilde began his professional career. The ensuing scandal forced him to seek a foreign transfer to PSV, of Holland.

In a separate incident, the fiery star attacked and injured a hospital nurse when he tried to enter the emergency room where his father was being treated for heart problems. As part of the sentence, he was ordered by the court to do community service, teaching soccer in poor neighbourhoods.

The 29-year-old had been in and out of the national team while the scandal was in full flow. Former coach Georges Leekens eventually lost patience. But his successor, Robert Waseige, reacting to a shortage of quality strikers, is impressed that De Bilde seems to have got his act together – and that his move to Wednesday seems to be a clean chapter in a life of someone who has matured at last.

He has always been known for his combative style – he takes no prisoners when he goes for the ball. Yet that masks an undoubted talent, his ability to score goals out of nothing as well as those requiring more brute force. Perhaps his closely-shaven head adds to the fearsome impression he creates. De Bilde won his first cap against Macedonia in November 1994 and was actually suspended when PSV signed him in 1997 from Anderlecht.

Hillsborough was not totally alien territory to De Bilde – he had been a big fan of English football and had long believed that his physical style was perfect for the Premiership. And he already knew one member of the Owls team – his old PSV clubmate, Dutchman Wim Jonk. They have worked well in harness since De Bilde's arrival, despite Danny Wilson's side's problems last season in the Premiership.

Holland and Belgium are, of course, joint hosts of Euro2000 and the teams have been seeded not to meet until at least the semi-final. De Bilde says: "Wim and I are hoping it will be in the final itself. There would be a lot of interest in Sheffield at least if that happens!"

Euro2000 verdict: Will we see the beauty of The Beast?

STATS

Born: 9 June 1971, Brussels.

Club: Sheffield Wednesday.

Fee: £3m from PSV Eindhoven, July 1999.

QUOTE

"Trouble seems to follow the man known as The Beast."

DID YOU KNOW?

He was Belgium Footballer of the Year in 1994.

RONALD DE BOER

MIDFIELDER

It is hard for a Dutch footballer as talented as Ronald De Boer to live with 1988. That, you see, is the equivalent of England's 1966. It was the year Holland won their only major international honour. De Boer and his twin brother Frank have had to live with the images of Ruud Gullit lifting the Henri Delauney Cup – that's the European Championship trophy to you and me – and try to add another glorious chapter in Dutch football history.

The endless comparisons with stars of yesteryear are difficult. But then the men from Orange know that their last golden generation may just be coming to the point of complete maturity and that now, on home soil, Euro2000 can provide a whole new set of images for Dutch football fans to feast on.

"There is some pressure from playing at home, of course, of being co-hosts. But then there are some advantages, too, and we must balance everything," says De Boer.

Holland go into every tournament as many people's second-choice team. They play with imagination and passion. They take on the established sides, like Germany and Italy, Argentina and Brazil, with no fear. But, too often, internal strife undermines their chances of success.

That was evident in Euro96 in England, where Edgar Davids was sent home following a row with coach Guus Hiddink, and the fall-out saw the Dutch annihilated 4-1 by rampant England at Wembley.

Ronald De Boer started every match in Holland's disappointing campaign. And he featured as the Dutch delighted but ultimately just failed to reach the last World Cup final.

"Both were huge disappointments," recalls the Barcelona star. "We must work hard with coach Frank Rijkaard to make sure things go right this time."

Rijkaard, of course, is a link to that 1988 team. "He has won it and we hope that experience will rub off for us," says De Boer.

Ronald has been slower to reach the peak of his craft than twin Frank, but he has his admirers. In 1998, Arsenal came calling. He was tied to Ajax and could not move. Barcelona persisted and the twins moved to Spain as a bulk purchase in 1999 – but only after they went on strike!

They were tied to long contracts and, initially, were refused the chance to move.

So the brothers stayed at home, training by themselves with small games of soccer-tennis in the garden. It could not go on.

De Boer is sad that it came to such a sorry end, given that he had been with Ajax since he was a young boy. He and Frank were graduates of the club's famed youth academy that has produced so many players in the national team. In 1991, Ronald was sold to Twente Enschede before returning a couple of years later to win domestic and European Cup honours with a formidable Ajax side.

Ronald began his career as a striker but is now comfortable in his familiar midfield role, often linking with central defender Frank's passes from the back. He gets forward effectively, as he demonstrated with goals against South Korea and Mexico in the World Cup. He also scored on his debut for Holland, against San Marino in 1993.

How he'd love to do the same in the final this summer...

Euro2000 verdict: He's one of Holland's twin towers!

STATS

Born: 15 May, 1970, Hoorn, Holland.

Club: Barcelona.

Fee: £8m from Ajax, June 1999.

QUOTE

"There is pressure as hosts - but we can win Euro2000."

DID YOU KNOW?

He scored on his Dutch debut againsts San Marino in 1993.

SEBASTIAN DEISLER

MIDFIELDER

German football fans have been bemoaning their lack of genuine young talent for almost ten years. The production line that produced genuine world-class stars, such as Lothar Matthaus, Jurgen Klinsmann, Steffen Effenberg and Matthias Sammer, appeared to have all but dried up.

There have been a few exceptions, like Lars Ricken, who tormented Manchester United in Borussia Dortmund's Champions' League semi-final success a few seasons ago.

'Where are the stars?' has been the fans' cry. Well, they may have found one at last in Sebastian Deisler.

'The Deis Man Cometh' might be a suitable headline if this young Hertha Berlin star gets his chance to shine in Euro2000. He's just 20 but is German football's Great White Hope. What's more, it has been a whirlwind rise to stardom for a youngster who was languishing on the subs' bench at faded giants Münchengladbach.

Barely 18 months ago he had yet to start a Bundesliga game. But the midfielder soon became the hottest property in the league.

They got on to his trail after he starred for the German Under-18s side that finished runners-up in the European Championship. He played with maturity beyond his young years and the phones at Gladbach, where he had been none too highly regarded, began to buzz.

The offers rolled in and cash-strapped Gladbach, who were once a major power with players such as Gunter Netzer, a European title winner with Germany in 1972, gratefully took the money.

Deisler took his chance as Gladbach headed for relegation. He shone despite the team's struggling form and relegation sealed his future, with the club forced to cash in on him in an effort to regain their First Division status.

Real Madrid and AC Milan were reportedly on Deisler's trail. The youngster's astute management decided that he wasn't ready for such a big step up in grade and settled instead for Hertha, who qualified for the Champions' League by finishing third in the Bundesliga.

It was a wise move, as Chelsea fans can testify. Deisler's pace and vision helped set up the Iranian, Ali Daei, who scored twice as unfancied Hertha beat the Blues 2-1 in Berlin. And he got another chance to impress his Milan admirers when Hertha drew 1-1 at the San Siro to go top of their group.

Deisler has been described as having the passing ability of former icon Netzer and the vision of Wolfgang Overath, a star of West Germany's 1966 World Cup team. He is, like David Beckham, being used wide on the right but groomed for a central midfield role. Like Beckham, too, he possesses a handy line in free-kicks.

Germany's coach, Erich Ribbeck, has invested a huge amount of faith in Deisler, believing he can come through into the side for the Championship finals.

The youngster missed a couple of the qualifiers through injury, but Ribbeck believes he already knows enough to have few doubts that Deisler can become German football's millennium babe...

Euro2000 verdict: A name to watch out for this summer.

STATS

Born: 5 January, 1980 Lorrach, Germany.

Club: Hertha Berlin.

Previous club: B. Münchengladbach.

QUOTE

'Seb is German football's Great White Hope.'

DID YOU KNOW?

His nickname in Germany is Das Super Talent.

Continental

ALESSANDRO DEL PIERO

STRIKER

This is one Del Boy who says there are many things in life money can't buy. You'd think life would be lubbly jubbly for someone earning a mind-boggling £70,000 a WEEK. The world should be his lobster, as the *Only Fools and Horses* star might say.

But the golden boy of Juventus is no fool. He is street-wise enough to know that 'money is important because it helps you live better but there are lots of things in life that it simply cannot buy'. Like carving a lasting impression on the international stage in the way that Del Piero has done at club level.

It grieves him that he has yet to make a lasting step up in class. However, at only 25, the best years of his career should still be in front of him.

Whether they will be spent at Juventus is another thing entirely. The Turin giants are known for turning over their star strikers with alarming regularity. Just ask Christian Vieri, Roberto Baggio, Alen Boksic, Fabrizio Ravanelli. Even Gianluca Vialli, who went from European Cup-winning Juve star to Chelsea striker in a matter of weeks.

Del Piero has scored more goals in the Champions' League than any other player since the competition was launched. It was the perfect platform for someone who can conjure the unexpected. At international level, though, Ice Man Alex has yet to be truly inspired.

At Juve, it was his partnership with Pippo Inzaghi that, for a time at least, dominated Serie A and frightened foreign defences. Del Piero is an unselfish provider, who can top up his tally of goals from wicked dead-ball strikes around the edge of the penalty box. He is a lethal finisher, with a range from tap-in to 30-yard curler over the top of the best-prepared defensive wall.

Del Piero's big problem when it comes to swapping the black and white of Old Lady Juve for the famous Azurri of his country, has been the man he recently overtook as the world's most moneyed player, Christian Vieri. Vieri was the star of the last World Cup, with five memorable strikes before Italy's premature departure from the competition, around the time of his £31m world-record transfer from Spain's Atletico Madrid to Juventus's big rivals Inter Milan, to team up with Ronaldo.

Italy's coach, Dino Zoff, a World Cup-winning captain in 1982, has preferred the Vieri-Inzaghi combination as his front pairing. But they scarcely distinguished themselves in the latter part of their Group One qualification battles, in which they topped the section by just a point, losing 3-2 to Denmark and drawing 0-0 in Belarus to stagger across the line. Indeed, Del Piero was thrown on in place of Vieri in Belarus when it became clear their seemingly unassailable lead at the top of the section was becoming less secure. Nevertheless, even Italy's golden boy could not break the deadlock.

Injuries have interrupted Del Piero's electric progress in recent seasons. He should have been fresh for France98 after an earlier knock, but failed to fizz. Knee ligament damage ruined his Champions' League hopes the season after that.

It was while he was on the sidelines that he dusted off his old contract, started talking about the new whopper, and reminded himself of his endorsements with Coca-Cola, Adidas and Disney, to name but three.

He was the crock who cracked it, you could say... but the highest accolade of his worth was that Juventus were prepared to break the bank to keep him, rather than show him the door.

Euro2000 verdict: If he gets the nod from Zoff, Del Boy will be Vieri delighted...

STATS

Born: 9 November, 1974, Conegliano.

Club: Juventus.

Previous club: Padova.

QUOTE

'Juventus broke the bank to keep Ice Man Alex.'

DID YOU KNOW?

Tactical blunders meant he played only 45 mins at Euro96.

MARCEL DESAILLY

DEFENDER

Marcel Desailly is a colossus – a multi-talented World Cup winner whom any manager or coach would give his right arm to sign. Chelsea's Gianluca Vialli only had to give up his hair!

Well, not quite. Vialli's bald dome is his trademark, but he has had occasion recently to tear out what hair he might have had because of Desailly. In particular, the Chelsea boss was upset with the French FA for selecting Desailly for their crucial final qualifier against Iceland in Paris, with their place in Euro2000 in doubt.

Desailly was carrying an injury and the Blues felt their Champions' League campaign was more important. This is the sort of confrontation that is going to become a growing feature of the game. Clubs pay the players' wages and resent them being injured on international duty.

Desailly reported to the French headquarters armed with a note from the Chelsea medical staff saying he would be unfit to face Iceland because of a groin injury. But the French called in their own doctor and Desailly was pronounced fit enough to play – as he did, in a dodgy 3-2 win.

Marvellous Marcel remained the perfect professional through it all, simply wanting to win every game. "It was a very tight group, perhaps the closest of all. I can understand the rows," he said. "We have a great spirit in this squad and had to come through some difficult games to reach the finals.

"It will be very demanding to follow up our victory in the World Cup, especially as we have a tough group with Holland, the Czechs and Denmark. When you are the world champions, much is expected of you. But it also brings confidence and we believe in ourselves much more since winning the World Cup."

Desailly is hugely popular as a double Champions' League winner, with Marseilles and AC Milan. A European crown would complete a unique set for this superb athlete.

When Chelsea came out for the warm up before their Champions' League game in Milan last season they must have thought they were about to play a testimonial for Desailly. For, at one end of the ground was a huge banner for him and he had to run the length of the field to acknowledge the cheers – from fans whose team he was about to play against!

Milan's fans, like those who will be following France at the finals this summer, know what a committed player Desailly is – and how essential he has been to every team for whom he has played. Yet he is also modest, saying: "I know I am not one of the greatest talents but I give my team everything. I play with my heart all the time."

His future at Chelsea will always be the subject of speculation, as he is desired by so many rival clubs. But he says: "It really lifts me when I see youngsters wearing a Chelsea shirt with my name on their back. That has never happened to me before. That is the sort of thing that makes you want to stay at a club." That comment has been at odds with reports of him leaving the club this summer.

Now, though, his thoughts turn to the Low Countries – and another major high point in his career. Victory really would etch Desailly's name in the all-time hall of fame.

Euro2000 verdict: Desailly aims to complete his trophy cabinet.

STATS

Born: 7 September, 1968, Accra, Ghana.

Club: Chelsea.

Fee: £4.6m from AC Milan, July, 1998.

QUOTE

"Winning the World Cup has given us more confidence."

DID YOU KNOW?

He could have played his football for Ghana, where he was born.

DIDIER DESCHAMPS
MIDFIELDER

Didier Deschamps has experienced that unique moment for a footballer – lifting the greatest prize in the game as captain of his country. And the man once famously criticised by Manchester United icon Eric Cantona as 'a water-carrier' says no-one can ever take that away from him, no matter what else he achieves before he hangs up his boots.

France's victorious skipper in the last World Cup is also one of a small, exclusive band of players to have won the Champions' League with two different clubs. He did it with Marseilles in 1993 and again with Juventus in 1996. His move to Chelsea last summer was a major surprise, signalling that his best days might be behind him.

But the Blues have gained from having someone with his calm authority at the heart of the side and his understanding with Marcel Desailly, a club-mate first at Marseilles and now at Stamford Bridge, is an important one.

It is important also for the French team. He led by example during Euro2000 qualifying games, especially when France at one point slipped to fourth place in their section.

The £3m Blues midfield anchorman went into the final matches on a caution, knowing that one slip meant he could miss the crucial closing game with Iceland, which France would need to win to qualify without having to go through the play-offs. "In those situations, you have to play your own game. You have to keep up your level of aggression, take the risks and hope for the best. Otherwise you cannot be effective. It is the same in all these group competitions.

"We did very well to take six points from our last two matches to qualify automatically. We might not have been at our best, but we got the result. Victory was all that mattered.

"It was a bit like the World Cup. We might not have played the prettiest football at times, especially early on. But we did what was necessary and went on to win the trophy.

"That was wonderful – the greatest day of my career. But I will be no less happy if we can win the European Championship. Then there can be no doubts that we are the best team in the world."

He says that the year following the World Cup was the most difficult – the sense of anti-climax was enormous. And that undermined France's start to qualifying for Euro2000. But coach Roger Lemerre still has much the same squad to select from – as well as some exciting younger players. "We will be hard to beat," says Deschamps.

It is more than ten years since Deschamps made his international debut, against Yugoslavia. He's now 32 and knows that this could be his last major finals. Because of injuries, the last World Cup was his first.

"It would be quite something to play in two major finals and win them both," he says.

"This will be a very difficult competition, a very open one. So much can happen. We just have to hope we get there with no major injuries and everyone in peak form.'

Euro2000 verdict: Deschamps de champ! A super player.

STATS

Born: 15 October, 1968, Nantes.

Club: Chelsea.

Fee: £3m from Juventus, July 1999.

QUOTE

'I want to win so there is no doubt we are the best team in the world.'

DID YOU KNOW?

He missed the Euro96 semi-final with an ankle injury.

adidas

YOURI DJORKAEFF

MIDFIELDER

The Serpent, they called him at Inter Milan. That's because French World Cup winner Youri Djorkaeff has this uncanny knack of finding his way without detection into deadly positions before striking.

Djorkaeff shone during the Euro2000 qualifying campaign while his more celebrated international team-mate Zinedine Zidane sat out much of it with injury. He looked to be a man with confidence renewed and certainly he is enjoying life away from Italy, having joined German club Kaiserslautern last summer.

British football fans got a few sights of the Armenian-born Djorkaeff in last season's UEFA Cup. First the Germans put aside the challenge of Kilmarnock, for whom star Gary Holt had promised to 'kick him all over the pitch'. But the masterful Frenchman proved too elusive and scored a typical brilliant free-kick in the leg in Scotland.

Then it was Tottenham, and Djorkaeff missed the first leg at Spurs after being injured in a domestic defeat by Bayern Munich. Ironically Spurs had been in the queue for Djorkaeff's signature in the summer, along with Atletico Madrid and Real Betis of Spain. Chelsea had sounded him out, too.

Spurs midfielder Steffen Freund is a big fan of Djorkaeff, who had been a big hit at Inter until finding himself less in demand in his last days at the club.

Freund says: "Youri is very good on the ball and can read the game so well. He is a very dangerous player and you have to man-mark him to keep him quiet.

"But then France have other dangerous midfield players, so it is not easy when you play them."

Freund is not surprised by Djorkaeff's instant impact with the former German champions. "He will do well anywhere and will be a big threat this summer."

Youri is the son of Jean Djorkaeff, a centre-back who was capped 48 times for France. "My father was a big influence on my career," says Djorkaeff junior.

He began his career at Grenoble and then Strasbourg before five successful seasons at Monaco raised his profile. Paris St. Germain lured him to the capital and, in 1995, they won the Cup-winners' Cup, beating Rapid Vienna in Brussels in Vienna, using a four-man strike force led by Djorkaeff.

With Zidane well below par in Euro96, it was Djorkaeff who stole the limelight for a French side that was beaten in the semi-finals by the Czech Republic, but which gave little indication they would rule the world two years later.

Naturally the Serpent was called upon to use his slippery skills in the World Cup, but his only strike there was from the penalty spot in a second-round win over Denmark.

He was on target, though, in the crucial 3-2 home win over Iceland that secured France's place at Euro2000.

Djorkaeff is now 32, so there are not too many big tournaments ahead for him. But don't doubt his motivation after the World Cup success of two years ago. "I still have the hunger," he warns.

Euro2000 verdict: This serpent may be just too long in the tooth...

STATS

Born: 9 March, 1973, Lyon, France.

Club: Kaiserslautern.

Previous club: Inter Milan, July 1999.

QUOTE

"I still have the hunger after our World Cup win."

DID YOU KNOW?

They called Youri 'The Serpent' at Inter Milan.

LJUBINKO DRULOVIC

MIDFIELDER

The Slavs have produced some wonderfully gifted players down the years. Sadly for domestic fans, they have to move abroad to win things.

For the players themselves it is a chance to experience new cultures, reap rich rewards and make friends for life. For Ljubinko Drulovic, moving to Portugal opened his eyes. An initial spell with little club Gil Vicente gave him a gentle introduction to life in the West. But his move to Porto was the making of him.

"I discovered a fantastic new world," he recalls. "Porto were former world and European champions. They had fantastic ambition and everything was geared for success." Five League championships are testimony to that, along with two Portuguese Cups.

It was in the summer of 1993 that he made the move from Gil Vicente. The 31-year-old Yugoslavian wide man was an instant hit, finishing second in the Portuguese goal charts in his first season, just three behind the Nigerian World Cup striker Rachidi Yekini.

Porto didn't win the league that season, remarkably, but the learning process for Drulovic was complete. Five straight titles followed as Porto left fierce rivals Benfica in their wake. He has since scored getting on for 50 goals for his club, though he is highly prized as a provider. His passing and crossing are of international class and he was heavily involved in Yugoslavia's Euro2000 qualifying campaign that was disrupted by the Kosovo crisis.

Porto team-mate Rui Barros describes Drulovic as 'an artist with the ball'. He makes things happen. Yugoslavia, though, have often been satisfied to use him from the bench. He is a versatile performer, operating wide on the left, where he can provide the bullets for his strikers. With Porto, that invariably means the prolific Brazilian Jardel. Yugoslavia look to Predraj Mijatovic and former Aston Villa striker Savo Milosevic for goals and they are rarely disappointed.

Drulovic made his international bow in 1996 against Argentina and has scored just once in almost 25 games for his country. He was in their squad for the last World Cup but did not play.

Rui Barros says: "I don't know why he doesn't get more games for Yugoslavia. His work rate is fantastic. He buzzes around, works really hard – he's absolutely indispensable to the team at Porto."

Drulovic is a little disappointed that the Slavs haven't been drawn in the same group as Portugal. "Perhaps that will be the final," he says, cheekily.

They have instead been paired with Spain – and the Porto fans will not be too disappointed if Drulovic and his team-mates can see them off. The sides clash in Bruges in the final game of Group C on June 21. With the hard-to-break-down Norwegians and tricky Slovenes in the same section, both might need a result from that one.

Might Drulovic join the travelling Slavs at the end of the tournament, though? So many move on throughout Europe at regular intervals. But he says not in his case, as the life in Portugal suits him and his family. The locals have always been welcoming and he has no desire to give it all up.

Euro2000 verdict: One to Drul over...

STATS

Born: 11 September, 1968, Belgrade.

Club: FC Porto.

Joined from: Gil Vicente (Portugal).

QUOTE

"He is absolutely indispensable at Porto."

RUI BARROS

DID YOU KNOW?

He made his debut in a 3-2 win over Argentina in 1996.

revigr
11

STEFAN EFFENBERG

MIDFIELDER

Stefan Effenberg is the one-time bad boy of German football who is now its biggest domestic icon and highest earner. The Bayern Munich midfielder led his club to the German championship and the Champions League final in 1999, in which they suffered a heartbreaking late defeat by Manchester United. And, while he has not featured so prominently in coach Erich Ribbeck's plans since the beginning of the Euro2000 qualifying, Germany's press and fans have been clamouring for his return to a side short of genuine quality, especially in midfield.

In 1992, he was a member of the side beaten by Denmark in the Euro final.

Two years ago, Effenberg was playing the best football of his career. At 32 this year, this could be his last major competition. The man whose career with Borussia Münchengladbach and Italian stars Fiorentina had been strewn with rows with coaches, team-mates and the press, had apparently reformed his behaviour, toed the line after a stern talking-to by Bayern chief Franz Beckenbauer, and finally showed the extent of the talent he possesses.

Effenberg was at his brilliant best in the Champions' League final, when Mario Basler gave Bayern an early lead and they were unlucky not to put the game beyond the Reds' reach. Such form made him an automatic choice in a European football writers' team of the season, alongside the likes of David Beckham, Jaap Stam and Gabriel Batistuta.

Effenberg is often labelled as arrogant and reserves such moments of humour as he may enjoy for times away from the public eye. He is, reportedly, his country's highest-paid player on £48,000 a week. That's before bonuses. And after tax.

But, he says, with the security of someone on the kind of money topped by few players in the world game, "I think only of winning. Nothing else.

"Still, if we don't then life will go on. Winter will come, then spring, then summer" – all very much in the image of Eric Cantona at his most inspiring and bemusing.

Perhaps, with Cantona a fading memory as a player, Effenberg believes this is a void he has to fill. He has none of the Frenchman's instant appeal, though plenty of the United legend's swagger.

His touch and vision compare with Cantona at his best and there is little doubt that Ribbeck would be foolish to ignore Germany's most gifted player this summer. The coach's only doubts are Effenberg's prickly personality, which may be ideally suited to Bayern – often known as Hollywood FC for the off-field dramas that have littered the club in recent times.

But being locked away for up to a month with the national squad might prove too much at a time when the coach is sure to be under huge pressure to produce results befitting a German international team in a major tournament.

Euro2000 verdict: Stefan's a star – but a potentially destructive influence.

STATS

Born: 2 August 1968, Germany.

Club: Bayern Munich.

Joined from: Borussia Münchengladbach, July 1998.

QUOTE

“I think only of winning. Nothing else.”

DID YOU KNOW?

He is Germany's highest-paid player, on £48,000 a week.

LUIS ENRIQUE

MIDFIELDER

Luis Enrique wears his heart not so much on his sleeve as on his trademark baseball cap which, away from the football arena, he uses to cover his closely-cropped head. 'No Fear', is the motto he carries. It sums up his attitude so well to the game that has brought him fame and fortune.

This is a man who outvoted even the great Brazilian Rivaldo in a national poll to find the best player in the Spanish League. He is also someone rated by Real Madrid legend Alfredo di Stefano as Spain's greatest all-rounder. Yet, Luis Enrique has a relatively low profile outside his native country – unless you have followed Barcelona's exploits in the Champions' League on mainstream TV, or the Primera Liga on satellite or cable.

He has none of the showiness of his Barca team-mate Rivaldo, but he has a certain swagger about him, a kind of assured air that colleagues look to when he lines up in the side. And no matter where he plays – for Luis Enrique has had a series of different roles for club and country – you can be sure he is an opponent of whom you should never lose sight.

Former Spanish national coach Javier Clemente was a huge fan of Luis Enrique. "If he was a girl, I'd marry him," he once said, famously. The new coach, Jose Antonio Camacho, is just as big an admirer of the man who loves to wear the No. 21 shirt – though not so embarrassing in his praise!

Luis Enrique is one of a rare breed in that he has played for Spain's two arch-rivals. Too often consigned to the subs' bench at Real Madrid, he jumped at the chance to join Barcelona in 1996 when his contract ran out.

He has been employed as a right-sided midfielder, in the 'hole', behind two front players and even in place of Albert Ferrer – now at Chelsea – as a right wing-back.

He is confident that Spain will at last live up to their promise when they go to the Low Countries this summer. He still recalls the pain and shame of the last World Cup when they failed to get past the group stage.

"We always said our group was wide open," he says. "Nigeria did not surprise us, but it was a big shock to go out, especially when we won our last game, against Bulgaria, 6-1. All the goals, all our efforts, counted for nothing because Paraguay beat Nigeria to go through in place of us.

"But we have only ourselves to blame and the real disappointment only sank in much later," he says.

Luis Enrique, now 29, has at least known what it is like to be on the top rung with the national team. He played in the side that won Olympic gold in Barcelona in 1992.

"We know we can win a major competition – the Olympics proved that, and it was a very proud day for us. Many of that side have remained in the squad – we have grown up together – and that is a reason to be confident.

"But we also know that our good record in qualifying counts for nothing when we get there. We all start on zero and there must be no slip-ups from the beginning."

Euro2000 verdict: Semi-finals a possibility for fired-up Luis Enrique.

STATS

Born: 8 April, 1970, Gijon.

Club: Barcelona.

Signed from: Real Madrid, June 1996.

QUOTE

"If he was a girl, I'd marry him."

JAVIER CLEMENTE

DID YOU KNOW?

He has played for both Real Madrid and Barcelona.

21
21

LUIS FIGO

MIDFIELDER

Luis Figo is the twinkle-toed genius who deserves to be a winner. If you've watched him in action leading Barcelona in the Champions' League, or saw his talent on show in a recent international for Portugal at Wembley, then you'll know what a talent he is.

Sadly for Figo – Luis Filipe Madeira Figo to give him his full name – some of his team-mates have seldom quite measured up to provide him with the level of success that should have come his way. That is more true at international level, with Portugal unable to build on the 'golden generation' of talent that came through ten years ago, winning successive World Under-20 Championships. Figo was even a member of the side that won the under-16 final in 1989. Figo joined Sporting Lisbon at 13 and played 124 league games for them. He moved to Barcelona in 1995 and scored the extra-time Spanish Cup winner in 1998.

Barcelona have had a measure of success, particularly on the home front, and any side with Figo and the brilliant Brazilian Rivaldo on board is some outfit. But even the Spanish giants have not been to the forefront of European glory.

David Seaman knows what it is to be on the end of Figo's genius. He knows, too, that England's 3-0 defeat of Portugal in a pre-1998 World Cup friendly at Wembley was in large part down to his brilliant first-half show in a spell dominated by Figo.

England were pushed back by Figo's sheer quality, highlighted by one sublime moment. After laying off to Pinto, Figo burst between Tony Adams and Gary Neville to take the return, and, spotting Seaman off his line, clipped the ball over him. It looked sure to become one of Wembley's greatest goals but, with Seaman helpless, it dropped a fraction wide.

"I remember being completely helpless – and relieved when it dropped safe," says Seaman, who renews his rivalry with Figo – capped almost 100 times for Portugal – when the sides meet in Eindhoven in a Group A clash on June 12 – both teams' opening match of the finals.

Seaman made two other superb saves from Figo that day, and the scoreline was very flattering to an England side then coached by Glenn Hoddle.

"Portugal showed they are a dangerous side and much of what they do revolves around Figo, so we'll need to keep him quiet," says Seaman.

Gary Neville had another sight of Figo during Manchester United's epic Champions' League battles with Barcelona a couple of years back. "He's very tricky – a dangerous opponent," concedes Neville.

The quality of Portugal's players – at Euro96 they were toasted as the 'Brazilians of Europe' – has never been in doubt, but they have often flattered only to deceive. Not Figo – he always produces a special bit of magic on the big occasion. And Kevin Keegan will have to have a special plan if the best Portuguese player of his generation is not to derail England's Euro campaign at the first hurdle.

Euro2000 verdict: One of the most dangerous players England face in their opening group.

STATS

Born: 4 November, 1972, Lisbon.

Club: Barcelona.

Joined from: Sporting Lisbon, June 1995.

QUOTE

"He's very tricky - a really dangerous apponent."

GARY NEVILLE

DID YOU KNOW?

Luis was a world champion at under-16 and under-20 level.

TORE-ANDRE FLO

STRIKER

Tore-Andre Flo, who led Norway's World Cup98 campaign and spearheaded their successful qualifying march to Euro2000 after a faltering start, has been urged to quit Chelsea by Norway's coach, Nils Semb.

The reason is that Chelsea haven't been going with the Flo often enough as manager Luca Vialli rotates his squad players.

Semb says: "Tore is my Number One striker and I advised him to leave Chelsea if they carried on using him as a substitute. He's a top-class international and doesn't deserve to be left on the bench. It's wrong for Vialli to leave out the best striker most of the time."

While Semb's words were unlikely to change Vialli's determination to keep on rotating the stars in his Blues' line-up to get the best out of them, there is little doubt that Flo, bought from Brann Bergen for a bargain £300,000, is one of the first names on his country's team sheet.

Flo, 6ft 4ins, signed a new five-year deal with Chelsea last summer and the £10m-rated striker would have sparked a stampede of clubs after his signature had he not been able to get the contract he wanted.

Vialli believes the big Norwegian has the potential to become a Stamford Bridge legend but had to work hard to persuade Flo that he would be a major part of the Blues' plans to conquer Europe.

It was the prospect of Champions' League football that helped to seal the decision, with Flo saying: "As a player you want to be the best and play against the best. The experience of playing against the best players in Europe can only help my game – at club level and for my country.

"I think my game has improved while I have been at Chelsea. It has been frustrating not being able to start every game. No player likes not to be involved. But sometimes you have to do what is best for the team."

Flo's goal against Brazil gave Norway a shock World Cup scalp, putting Scotland out of the competition in France. His likely starting partner for Norway is the young Valerenga prodigy, John Carew, and the pair will take some dislodging from the side if their duet works well. Both are prodigious scorers – Flo averages a goal every other game for his country. Carew is a giant, like Flo. He's known as Little John, despite being 6ft 4ins, and has played at every level for Norway, from under-15 to full international.

"John is an exciting prospect," says Flo, the youngest of three footballing brothers – Jostein and Havard Flo also ply their trade in England. "I can see him going a long way in the game."

But what about Norway's prospects in Euro2000, drawn against Spain, Yugoslavia and Slovenia? Flo says the Norsemen need fear no-one – and he'll be trying to get the low-down on Spain from Blues team-mate Albert Ferrer.

Euro2000 verdict: Flo will be a major handful for even the best defenders.

STATS

Born: 15 June, 1973, Strin, Norway.

Club: Chelsea.

Fee: £300,000 from Brann Bergen, August 1997.

QUOTE

"It's wrong for Chelsea to leave him out."

NILS SEMB

DID YOU KNOW?

Tore has played for Norway at every level since he was 15.

UMBRO
9

BJARNE GOLDBAEK

MIDFIELDER

Bjarne Goldbaek had no qualms about stepping down from the Premiership to join Mohammed Al-Fayed's mega-bucks Fulham squad. Playing First Division football at least meant regular first-team football. That had to be preferable to life on the bench at Chelsea – and the threat of that to his international place.

His £650,000 switch to Craven Cottage surprised many, especially when it seemed Goldbaek's destiny had taken him a mile or so up the road to Stamford Bridge.

After a career spent largely in Germany, with Schalke, Kaiserslautern and Koln, the 32-year-old joined FC Copenhagen in his native Denmark. It was when the Danes played Chelsea in Europe that the midfielder won wide acclaim, particularly for his performance and crucial away goal at the Bridge.

In just three weeks, he found his career turned upside down. When Brian Laudrup won the tie for Chelsea in Copenhagen, Goldbaek moved in the opposite direction to him, inherited Laudrup's No. 7 shirt – and then made two of Chelsea's five goals in a superb Blues Premiership debut at Arsenal.

"I did have to give some thought to coming over," he said at the time. "I would have had a free transfer at the end of that season and I had a choice of clubs to go to. Also, I had my wife and young son to consider.

"But it is not often in your career that you get such an offer from such a club, especially when you are over 30."

It all left Goldbaek breathless, though he can tackle Euro2000 with the confidence of having been involved with multi-national Chelsea's Champions' League campaign. And he'll have brought all that experience to bear in Fulham's assault on a Premiership place.

Goldbaek is an industrious right-sided midfield player. With Chelsea beset by injuries and suspensions, he fitted the bill at the Bridge, soon making his mark. He came off the bench at Sheffield Wednesday to lay on Roberto di Matteo's late winner in the FA Cup fifth round and, a week later, scored his first in the Premiership with two at Nottingham Forest.

He completed a dream start with a further strike against Liverpool and then against Aston Villa to make it four goals in as many games. A 30-yard thunderbolt at Tottenham, sadly too late to bring Chelsea any title joy, at least helped to book their third-place finish and a spot in the enlarged Champions' League.

Last season, though, Goldbaek didn't get too many chances to shine for the Blues. Boss Gianluca Vialli wanted to hang on to him, though Goldbaek suspected that it was only a matter of time before he would be shipped out of the Bridge.

The Dane turned down £2.5m moves to Birmingham and Nottingham Forest, and Vialli said he was happy for Goldbaek to stay. "We accepted Forest's offer and left the decision to Bjarne. At £350,000, he was a great bargain buy and did a great job. But I understood that he needed first-team football in order to keep his international place and could not promise that at Chelsea."

One downside to the move for Chelsea – and possible bonus for Fulham now – is that the Blues' Christmas party entertainment is sure to suffer. Last year, while Spaniard Albert Ferrer belted out 'La Bamba', Goldbaek stole the show with his version of 'Rudolf The Red-Nosed Reindeer' – in Danish!

He had apparently been taught the words by international team-mate Peter Schmeichel, who is well known for his red nose! Heaven k-nose what Goldbaek and chums have lined up should they win the big one in the Low Countries this summer...

Euro2000 verdict: Bjarne winner, this one.

STATS

Born: 6 October, 1968, Nykobing Falster.

Club: Fulham.

Fee: £650,000 from Chelsea, January 2000.

QUOTE

"He was a great bargain buy and did a great job for Chelsea."

GIANLUCA VIALLI

DID YOU KNOW?

'Red-nose' Bjarne stole the show at Chelsea's Christmas party.

7

RAUL GONZALEZ

STRIKER

Amazingly, Spain thumped eight goals past Cyprus to book their place at Euro2000 with a match to spare. After all, England coaches say there are no easy international games. Even more amazingly, the brilliant young Real Madrid hot-shot, Raul, didn't get one of them!

Mind you, Raul Gonzalez, to give him his full name, played his part. He had bagged his share of the booty as Spain plundered 42 goals in their qualifying cakewalk. And, when not on the scoresheet, Raul proved himself to be an unselfish provider.

Raul was only 17 when former Madrid coach Jorge Valdano called him up during an injury crisis at the Bernabeu Stadium. The youngster never looked back and was soon a fixture for the club as they won the Spanish title and then the Champions' League in 1998, the club's first success in that competition for 30 years.

He doesn't remember that earlier victory, of course. But Raul recalls his dad, an electrician, working round the clock, to keep food on the table for the family, in a poor Madrid suburb.

When it was discovered that Raul had a natural talent for football, the family diet was always going to improve. It did so rapidly.

He has seen off the experienced Croatian, Davor Suker, and Yugoslav Predraj Mijatovic to hold down a regular starting place at Real. Suker, of course, was the Golden Boot at the last World Cup and is now with Arsenal. Raul has been a fixture despite the arrival of £23m Nicolas Anelka from Highbury.

In the national side, Raul has had the company of his Madrid team-mate Fernando Morientes. Former coach Javier Clemente was an avid fan of Raul, promoting him as soon as he felt he was ready. His successor, Jose Antonio Camacho, has favoured the Athletic Bilbao pair, of Julen Guerrero and Ismael Urzaiz, but Raul has always been prominent in his squad selections.

With Spain winning praise in recent matches for showing a new-found pride, Raul's youthful hunger has been infectious throughout the team.

"We have an exciting new feel about the team," he says. "We could do very well in the finals." His enthusiasm has been known to spill over away from the game, however. Last autumn Camacho organised a small bullfight, using young calves. Raul and his Real skipper Fernando Hierro got involved in the event – even taking the cape at one point to put on a show.

Camacho soon had Madrid's bosses on the phone, blasting him for allowing their stars to put themselves at risk of injury. The lesson was learned and Camacho apologised.

Raul's proudest moment so far has come not on the football field but when he was able to buy his mother her own home. He is essentially an unassuming character, who likes the simple pleasures, such as reading, watching TV and listening to music.

Watching Raul in full flow is another of life's simple pleasures...

Euro2000 verdict: If Spain retain their form, he'll be the Raul McCoy...

STATS

Born: 27 June, 1977, Madrid.

Club: Real Madrid.

Fee: None.
Real Madrid junior.

QUOTE

"We have an exciting feel to the Spanish team now."

DID YOU KNOW?

Raul had his wrist slapped for trying his hand at bull fighting.

15
15
adidas

GHEORGHE HAGI

MIDFIELDER

You can't think of Romanian football without the image of little Gheorghe Hagi, all balletic grace and cleverness, either scoring a wicked goal from one touchline, or calling the shots from central midfield with a stern look on his face.

He's had a wonderfully exciting career – his international debut was against East Germany in 1983 – and achieved so much on the world stage. There is a certain sadness, though, as he nears retirement, that he didn't get to play in the English Premiership. It nearly happened, as he reflects while sipping coffee at the Galatasaray training centre not far from the heart of teeming Istanbul, the Turkish city that is his current home.

"'Yes," he confirms. "It was just after the World Cup in America. Things had gone well for Romania and we had reached the quarter-finals. We lost to Sweden on penalties, when really we should have won.

"But all round the world people could see the quality we had in our team and it was Tottenham who made a big effort to sign me. Ossie Ardiles was manager at the time. He was very keen for me to come to London and I gave it a lot of thought. But then Barcelona came in for me. That was a great opportunity, one I didn't want to miss. But Tottenham were close."

When his spell in Spain came to an end – he'd earlier played for Real Madrid – Newcastle later also tried to lure Hagi to England. Instead he opted for Istanbul, where he is revered almost as much as in his native Romania.

Last season was his farewell to club football. His dream of signing off by winning the Champions' League was probably a bit fanciful to say the least – Gala are good, but no giants of the European game.

But Hagi had hit the heights earlier in his exciting career, when he was the jewel in the crown of the much-admired Steaua Bucharest side, one of the best to have come from Eastern Europe. He won three league and cup doubles with Steaua (it means 'star').

As freedom came to Romania and mega-bucks were waved from abroad, the best Romanian stars, with Hagi at the top of the hit list, went abroad.

On the field, Hagi often plays with his face pulled into a tight scowl or grimace. The arms go round like windmills when decisions go the other way. He says: "When I am on the field, I play with an ugly face. But on the field, I am very serious, I have total concentration. I am very committed to winning. But, you see, I can look happy!

"I love football. It is very important to me, so that explains maybe how I look on the pitch. But I am not like that all the time."

Beaten twice on penalties in recent World Cups, the Romanians have not achieved as much as they have deserved. After appearing in all three World Cups in the 1990s, Euro2000 is Hagi's last chance to get it right. Stand by for fireworks...

Euro2000 verdict: Gheorghe boy will be sorely missed.

STATS

Born: 5 February 1965, Romania.

Club: Galatasaray.

Previous club: joined from Barcelona, July 1996.

QUOTE

"I play with an ugly face but I can be happy!"

DID YOU KNOW?

He is only the second Romanian to win 100 caps.

10
10

DIETER HAMANN

MIDFIELDER

Liverpool's German international midfielder Dieter Hamann steps into the breach this summer with a new belief that he might be the man to lift the defending European champions' fortunes.

Hamann has never doubted his own abilities through all sorts of trials, including a mental breakdown and a troublesome spell at Newcastle United, where he was cast aside by former manager Ruud Gullit and eventually sold by the Dutchman.

There was a time when his own confidence must have been stretched, with many observers convinced he might never play again after illness forced him out of football three years ago.

Now, though, with the German team in an unfamiliar state of unease, through the retirement of established stars and the failure to unearth enough new ones, Hamann could be the man of the moment.

He says: "Germany are going through a transitional phase and everyone feels that the future is very bleak for us. I don't see it that way.

"We have too many good players for that and just need a little more time to help Germany emerge as a real force again. I am keen to play my part.

"I know people have suggested that the coach, Erich Ribbeck, might base the team around me. It is nice to hear that and I am determined to justify his faith in me." Hamann adds: "It is never easy when a team loses so many long-established players. But I am sure we will get it right in the Low Countries."

He became Gerard Houllier's seventh and final signing of the summer of 1999 when finally getting his move from Newcastle. And he is intent on doing his bit for Liverpool on and off the field – with fellow German star Markus Babbel, of Bayern Munich, apparently lined up to join him at Anfield this summer.

Hamann's own £8m transfer to Anfield ended an unhappy spell at Newcastle, where he was fined £40,000 by Gullit for talking to Arsenal about a possible move. He had been signed by Kenny Dalglish for £5.5m. The Gunners then bid £7m for him and Hamann released a statement in Germany saying he believed his future lay with Arsene Wenger's team. But Hamann was rapped with a huge fine for talking to another team while still under contract with Newcastle.

He was influential for Germany during their qualifying campaign, although he came off at half-time in their crucial 0-0 draw with closest rivals Turkey following an ankle injury that had caused him problems last season. "I asked the coach to take me off. I was not doing myself justice," he said.

However, he believes both himself and the German team will do themselves justice this summer, and Hamann is eagerly looking forward to meeting England. The game may pit him against Liverpool midfield team-mate Paul Ince and striker Michael Owen. "That will be interesting, to say the least," he says.

"The game will be built up like very few others after all the past rivalries and with the prospect of further meetings in the World Cup qualifying group. It will be a difficult match to predict. But we should not ignore Romania or Portugal, who are both dangerous opponents," warns Hamann.

Euro2000 verdict: Didi can do the business for the holders.

STATS

Born: 27 August, 1973, Waldsasson, Germany.

Club: Liverpool.

Fee: £8m from Newcastle United, July 1999.

QUOTE

"Playing against England will be... interesting!"

DID YOU KNOW?

Dieter once suffered a nervous breakdown.

adidas
16
FIFA WORLD CUP
FRANCE 98
ION

MAGNUS HEDMAN

GOALKEEPER

Coventry City goalkeeper Magnus Hedman is something like the Becks of Swedish football – married to a pop-star wife. Not that you'd ever catch him wearing a sarong, let alone her underwear!

His wife, Magdalena, is actually more famous than him back in Scandinavia, though that might change if Sweden win Euro2000. If it has the sound of another David Beckham-Posh Spice pairing, Hedman is not one for the celebrity lifestyle, despite marrying Sweden's biggest pop star since Abba just six days before the qualifying win against Poland that gave England a back-door route to the finals.

Astonishingly, Hedman, aged 27, has only been a professional footballer for barely three years. Before that he was a marketing man with an economics degree and a dream to become a full-time footballer, playing in the Premiership.

It has all happened in a whirl and Hedman has brushed aside two long-established goalkeeping figures in order to achieve his dream. When Coventry paid AIK Solna £500,000 to take him to Highfield Road, Hedman took the No.1 shirt long possessed by Steve Ogrizovic. Oggy is a Sky Blues legend.

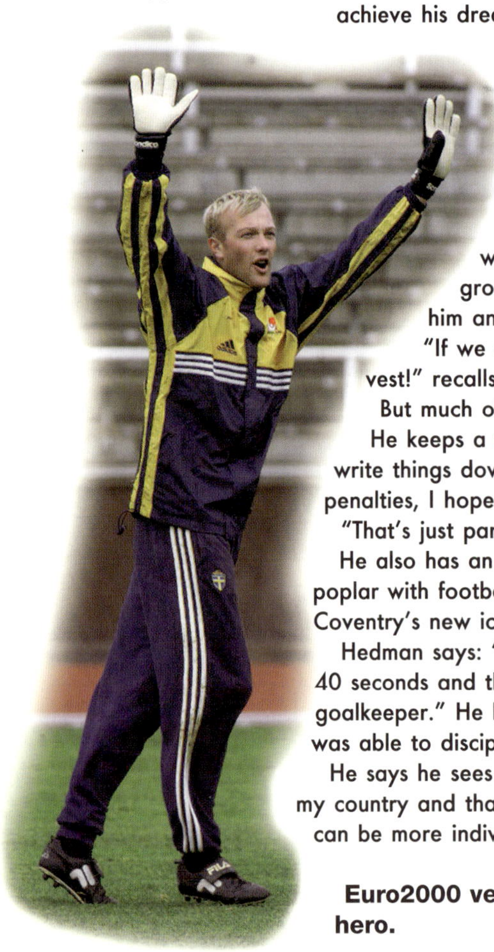

Then, after impressing Sweden coach Tommy Soderberg of his talent, Hedman replaced Thomas Ravelli, then the most-capped player in international football until Lothar Matthaus equalled his world-best total of 143 caps last autumn.

He knows the heat will be on for Sweden, who were impressive qualifiers, when the finals begin. They face Belgium, Turkey and Italy in the opening group. But he says he's used to pressure after that final qualifier that made him an England hero.

"If we didn't win, I was thinking of coming back to Coventry in a bullet-proof vest!" recalls Hedman, who kept 15 clean sheets in his first 20 internationals.

But much of this intelligent man's success is down to detailed forward planning. He keeps a database of opponents on his computer. "I like to study opponents and I write things down on my computer which I think are worth saving. When it comes to penalties, I hope to always have some kind of note.

"That's just part of being prepared, being professional in the game today," he says.

He also has an unusual preference for his days off-duty. Not for him the round of golf so poplar with footballers. He's an expert ice-hockey player and is a regular visitor to Coventry's new ice rink.

Hedman says: "It's good training for the legs. You have to give it everything on the ice for 40 seconds and then you rest. That's the same sort of activity as when you are a goalkeeper." He has also done martial arts, saying: "I was in advanced tai kwando and I was able to discipline my brain and my body."

He says he sees everything as a challenge. "I followed two famous keepers for my club and my country and that is also a test. But one of the reasons I like being a goalkeeper is that you can be more individual. I am either a hero or a villain."

Euro2000 verdict: If Sweden are the big surprises, Hedman could be their hero.

STATS

Born: 19 March, 1973, Stockholm.

Club: Coventry City.

Fee: £500,000 from AIK Solna, July 1997.

QUOTE

"I train on an ice rink to build up my legs."

DID YOU KNOW?

He uses a computer to help him save penalties.

ndico
adidas
1
sondico
SMG
Sondico
adidas

VEGARD HEGGEM

DEFENDER

Norwegian defender Vegard Heggem loves his home from home at Liverpool – and reckons England have as good a chance as any side in the competition of winning Euro2000.

But the £3.5m former Rosenborg star says he has even higher hopes for little Norway – and this is his big chance to put past disappointment behind him and enjoy life in the big-time to the full.

Heggem, a popular recruit at Anfield since signing from the Norwegian champions in the summer of 1998, was robbed of a chance to play in the World Cup because of a groin injury he picked up in the days before the finals in France two years ago.

He had made his international debut in the February of that year – and scored against World Cup hosts France in that friendly international. He thought he'd be able to make his mark in the finals, but injury robbed him of a chance to start a game, despite being handed the No.14 shirt in Norway's 22-man squad.

"It was cruel, yes, but you have to accept disappointment sometimes in football. It was sad to have to watch the finals from the bench, especially when we played Brazil – and beat them! That was a famous day for us, being a small country in football terms," he says.

"And it was no fluke. It showed how far we have progressed in recent years. Now we almost expect to qualify for major events."

Norway were beaten 1-0 by Italy in the second round but Heggem knew he would probably not have been fit even if they had reached the final itself.

His move to Liverpool was some consolation. And if he needed the low-down on Anfield, then he knew the right people to ask – Stig Bjornebye and Oyvind Leonhardsen, then both with Liverpool. The latter is now at Tottenham.

Heggem was much sought after by rival clubs and Roy Evans was delighted with his capture – one of his last before standing down as Reds' boss. Evans believes Heggem has proved him right since his move to Merseyside. "He is spot-on for the Premiership. He is good at delivering quality balls into the box, which is something you need when you have players as quick in there as Michael Owen and Robbie Fowler," says Evans.

He may not have Owen's blinding pace but, at 25, Heggem is approaching the peak of his powers and is ambitious to win things at club level and with his country. "We have a very good spirit in the national team. Of course, with so many of us playing in the Premiership we see each other quite a lot, too," he says.

"We have made a number of changes in the side but the new coach, Nils Semb, has drawn on the strength of Egil Olsen's squad. I think other teams will see us as a big threat.

"Denmark's win in 1992 showed that the smaller countries can compete at this level, and we are very much looking forward to the matches."

Euro2000 verdict: Vegard's the star of the Norwegian rearguard.

STATS

Born: 13 July, 1975, Trondheim, Norway.

Club: Liverpool.

Fee: £3.5m from Rosenborg, July 1998.

QUOTE

"Denmark showed small countries can win big prizes."

DID YOU KNOW?

Injury cost Vegard a chance to play in the World Cup.

UMBRO
7

THIERRY HENRY

STRIKER

France went into the last World Cup with real question-marks about where the goals would come from. Arsenal's Nicolas Anelka was too young and inexperienced, domestic hero Stephane Guivarc'h looked unable to hit a barn door from several yards out, and Christophe Dugarry was too inconsistent.

Zinedine Zidane was no Michel Platini – he would not score enough from midfield to bring the hosts the pot of gold on home soil.

Step forward Thierry Henry. The live-wire young winger seemed to be earmarked for a role as provider, but three goals in the group matches against South Africa, Denmark and Saudi Arabia was enough to underline the fact that major tournaments always unearth major talents.

'Titi' Henry, Arsenal's record buy of £11m from Juventus last year, could have been a sprinter. His 100-metre times as a youngster were exceptional. But his skill with the ball at his feet, allied to this pace, is what makes him a world beater – as France indeed were two years ago. His recent move to Highbury was a dream come true for Henry, who says he learned so much under Gunners boss Arsene Wenger when he was head coach at Monaco, Henry's former club.

"Henry has turbo-charged legs," says Wenger, who gave Henry his first team debut in the French League at just 17.

Henry first came to the attention of English supporters when he starred in Monaco's UEFA Cup tie against Newcastle in 1997 at St James' Park, where his pace set up a brilliant goal for Sonny Anderson.

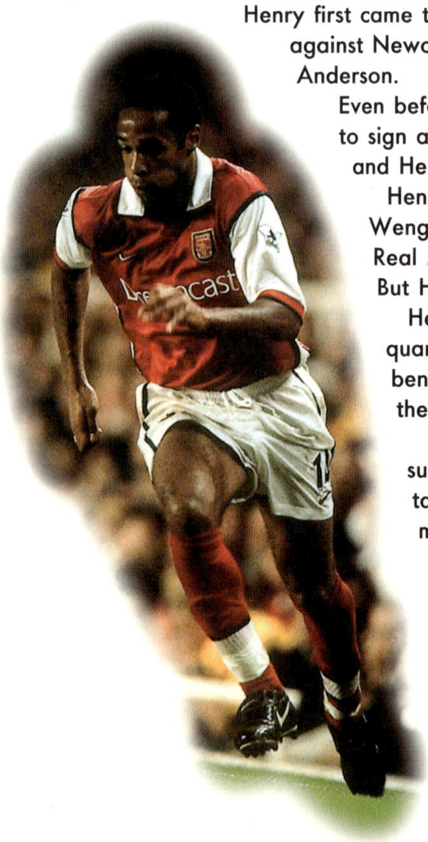

Even before the World Cup, Real Madrid beat off a posse of clubs to get the youngster to sign a pre-contract agreement. But, because of his age, the deal broke UEFA rules and Henry was left with a £40,000 fine.

Henry has the temperament to become a French hero for many years and, under Wenger's guidance, will surely emerge to fill the void left by Anelka's defection to Real Madrid a year ago. Both players have pace and there are obvious comparisons. But Henry doesn't want to be seen as Anelka Mark Two.

Henry showed he has the nerve for the big occasion, netting in the World Cup quarter-final penalty shoot-out win against Italy, though he had to come off the bench to play a part in the latter stages of the competition. And he didn't get on the field for the final itself, which is his greatest disappointment to date.

Henry did not feature too often in the qualifying tournament for Euro2000, surprisingly in the view of many, including Wenger. France remain short of natural talent in the striking department, particularly with Anelka suffering from lack of match appearances amid upheaval at Real Madrid last term.

Bordeaux's Sylvain Wiltord, who made his debut as a sub in a 2-0 Wembley win against England, and David Trezeguet do not look the answer. But if Henry shows the kind of form that Wenger was able to coax out of him last season, and the player learns from his close-quarters view of Dutch duo Dennis Bergkamp and Marc Overmars, he has the talent to rise to the occasion once again for his country.

Euro2000 verdict: Could be hooray Henry after the final...

STATS

Born: 17 August, 1977, Paris.

Club: Arsenal.

Fee: £11m from Juventus, 3 August, 1999.

QUOTE

‘Henry has turbo-charged legs.’

ARSENE WENGER

DID YOU KNOW?

Thierry could have been a world-class 100-metre sprinter.

adidas
12
12

FERNANDO HIERRO
MIDFIELDER

Fernando Hierro is living proof that iron can be worth its weight in gold. For Iron is the Real Madrid star's nickname. And it was earned because of the hard-man attitude he employs on the field. But do not be taken in by the idea that physical strength is Hierro's only asset. An adaptable defensive player, he is a more than capable prompter of things in midfield, with the ability to keep possession of the ball.

Hierro was never better than when Real lifted the Champions' League crown two years ago, against hot favourites Juventus. He was the dominant figure in the game.

Bobby Robson, the recently-appointed manager of Newcastle United, has fond memories of his time as coach at Barcelona. However, he recalls that Hierro always gave him nightmares when Barca played their fiercest domestic rivals.

"He is quite simply the best defender in the Spanish Primera Liga,' says the former England manager. "He is strong in the tackle. But he likes to get forward and can be a dangerous player to ignore around the edge of your own penalty box, as he can also score goals.

"He's a hard character, and is the wrong side of 30. But there's all that experience now and he will be a key player for Spain."

The Spanish were hugely disappointing at the last World Cup. And hugely disappointed at their Euro96 exit at the hands of England. Hierro recalls: "We were the better side against England and should have had a penalty. We also had a good goal disallowed. But it was never going to be easy for us playing the hosts at Wembley.

"As for the World Cup, I know a lot was expected of the team after Real beat Juventus but, to this day, I still can't understand why we under-performed."

The former Valladolid defender has benefited from playing a more forward role in recent seasons with Real. "It has helped me as a defender. Often I look into an attacker's eyes to see how he is going to take me on. Anticipation is three-quarters of the defender's art."

Real value Hierro enormously – clubs are warned off approaching the Madrid giants for his signature by the huge buy-out clause, some £21m, attached to his contract. And the player himself earns around £1.5m a year. He intends to see out his career with Real but his biggest remaining ambitions are to enjoy some success at last with Spain.

Too often in recent years they have breezed through the qualifying stages of major events, only to fail to deliver the big prize that many tip them to win. Spain were the most impressive of the qualifying nations this time, losing just once in eight starts and rattling up 42 goals after opening up with a shock 3-2 defeat in Cyprus.

A Hierro own-goal in Austria was one of only two other blemishes on the debit side and he made up for it by scoring at the other end in a decisive 3-1 win in Vienna.

Now Spain need to take that form to the Low Countries... with Iron Man keen to get his hand on that silver trophy.

Euro2000 verdict: Hierro will remain a Real hero, no matter what happens.

STATS

Born: 23 March, 1968, Malaga.

Club: Real Madrid.

Previous Club: Valladolid.

QUOTE

"He's the best defender in Spain. A hard man."

BOBBY ROBSON

DID YOU KNOW?

It will cost any admiring club £21m to buy his contract.

adidas
6

JES HOGH

DEFENDER

Jes Hogh's arrival at Chelsea was quite understated – with little of the fanfare that greeted many of the better-known imports. But he is no less a valued member of Gianluca Vialli's league of nations.

And Hogh is equally highly thought of as a member of the Danish international set-up – even if he wishes Peter Schmeichel would be struck down by laryngitis again!

Like any defender lining up in front of the former Manchester United keeper, Hogh, 33, is prone to getting an ear-bashing from Schmeichel.

His mind goes back to a blissful occasion when Hogh was with Fenerbahce, the Turkish club, drawn to play United in a Champions' League tie a few years back. Schmeichel had conceded a shocking 11 goals in consecutive Premiership defeats at Newcastle and Southampton. Hogh recalls feeling a bit sorry for the players in front of him at the time – Schmeichel yelled at them non-stop. And he added to United's worries as the Turks ended their proud record of never having lost a home European tie in 40 years.

"I remind Peter of that one from time to time," says Hogh. "He's a fantastic goalkeeper who has been a major figure in Denmark's recent successes – especially the 1992 European championship win – as well as all he did at United.

"But I'm glad I don't have to play in front of him every week!"

Hogh has been enjoying his time in the Premiership and knows this is likely to be his last major international tournament. He is a shrewd player, with strong opinions, who seems well suited to holding a managerial capacity after he hangs up his boots.

For instance, he believes that England will never again be a potent world force while they play fancy-dan European-style football. He says: "It baffles me why England try to do things they do not do in club football, things that don't come naturally."

Hogh says England should let Brazil play their way, Italians do their thing – and Kevin Keegan's men should play to their own strengths.

Denmark were called off beaches in 1992 to replace banned Yugoslavia – and promptly became European Champions. And Hogh says: "There was no secret to our success then or now. We played as a team and did the same things we did in club matches. "There was a time when opposing teams didn't like to play against England. Now when England play in Europe they try to play the European way – and usually lose.

"It is noticeable that only Manchester United win in Europe. It is because they play the same way as they do in the Premiership. England should do the same.

"The English game is pressure, physical. Never stop working. It is hard to play against. I should know because I am at Chelsea and have never played so many tough games.

"If England teams could keep the same pace and physical aggression as they do in the Premiership then few would touch them," he adds.

Euro2000 verdict: High Hogh silver lining.

STATS

Born: 7 May, 1966, Aalborg, Denmark.

Club: Chelsea.

Fee: £330,000 from Fenerbahce, July 1999.

QUOTE

"Team work is the secret to our success."

DID YOU KNOW?

He helped end Man United's proud home record in Europe.

hummel
4
DBU

ADRIAN ILIE

STRIKER

Sunderland manager Peter Reid wants to bring the Cobra to the Stadium of Light – and believes Romanian striker Adrian Ilie is one of the most dangerous players England will face in Euro2000. Ilie is aptly nicknamed, according to former England midfielder Reid. "It's a good nickname – but he reminds me more of a grass-snake. You don't see him – then all of a sudden you do and the ball's in the back of the net!"

In his native Craiova, Ilie was known as an arrogant performer and lethal goalscorer whom they labelled: 'The killer with the soul of a child'.

Reid recalls: "Ilie played against us for Steaua Bucharest in a testimonial for our defender Richard Ord. On the strength of what I saw that night, I tried to sign him – but he wanted to go to Spain. He is a quality player, and very quick."

Ilie elected to move to Valencia and had a huge impact, averaging a goal every other game. Mind you, he has a reputation for collecting yellow cards by the handful, too. But Reid loves that competitive edge about a striker.

At the World Cup, Ilie scored a brilliant goal against Colombia and played his part in the upset of England that helped the Romanians top their opening group.

He does have something of an abrasive manner, but Reid believes he could handle that. Ilie upset many Valencia fans not long after he arrived at the club, and Real Madrid bid £12m for him. He said: "If Real Madrid or Barcelona want me, I'm off." Angry supporters flooded the local radio station with calls after that incident.

Fans and team-mates alike have been quick to call him greedy, for failing to pass to others who might be better placed to score.

Ilie has succeeded Gheorghe Hagi as his country's superstar. Even Hagi agrees: "Adrian has always had talent – and now he has developed into a true star.

"He was always going to be one of the big names at the World Cup. And now he will continue to build his reputation this summer."

Romania fancy their chances of upsetting England yet again when the sides meet in the finals. Ilie, 25, who left Turkish club Galatasaray for Spain three years ago, loves playing against England and English clubs.

He starred in a UEFA Cup win over Liverpool two seasons ago. But he had to sit out Valencia's Champions' League date with Manchester United last season because of illness.

David Seaman is one who wouldn't mind Ilie to be in the stands when the sides meet again in Charleroi on June 20. The England keeper remembers the World Cup clash when he was almost embarrassed by Ilie's clever chip that struck the bar.

And Tony Adams, another who played in that game, says: "There is no doubt he is one of the best players in the world. He is sharp, quick and has a great left foot."

Back in Romania comes the warning that Ilie is still improving. Mercia Bendrea, who coached Ilie in his early years, says: "He is destined for greatness. Until now we have only scratched the surface."

Euro2000 verdict: Cobra packs venomous bite.

STATS

Born: April 22, 1974, Romania.

Club: Valencia.

Previous club: Galatasaray.

QUOTE

"Cobra? He reminds me more of a grass snake."

PETER RIED

DID YOU KNOW?

Ilie almost made David Seamen look silly at the World Cup.

adidas
11

FILIPPO INZAGHI

STRIKER

In the debate over who starts up front in the blue shirt of Italy, Filippo Inzaghi is the only winner. The Juventus striker seems to be the first name on coach Dino Zoff's team sheet and all the debate seems to be who will partner the brilliant young Juventus star.

Is it his Juve team-mate, the supremely gifted Alex Del Piero? Or the world's costliest player, Christian Vieri, of Inter?

The main rivals slug it out in Serie A each week, and each has his supporters in the media. But through it all, the man one critic labelled 'a gnome' has kept his opinions to himself and been the perfect professional. After all, he knows what it is like to be the odd man out. At the last World Cup, Inzaghi was behind Vieri in the pecking order under former coach Cesare Maldini.

Juve value Inzaghi highly. He cost them £9m three years ago after impressing the nation with 24 goals for a poor, struggling Atalanta side.

It took Inzaghi quite a while to become an overnight sensation. He began his career at Piacenza and was then sold to a Third Division outfit, Leffe, before getting back on track at Verona and, briefly, Parma.

Two years older than Del Piero, Inzaghi speaks highly of his Juventus strike partner. "He is a genius," he says. "He can make the impossible pass and always seems to be able to find a team-mate in traffic.

"Alex is clever around the penalty box. He makes space and he can get in crosses when defenders think he has no chance. We work very well together and he is often involved in the goals I score." English fans, unless watching Juve's exploits on TV, have not seen Inzaghi at his lethal best. He and Del Piero have the best record in Italian football since the 1960s, but when Inzaghi played at Wembley, in a World Cup qualifier in 1997, the senior partner was substituted.

Italy, though, won the match 1-0, so Inzaghi shed few tears. But that performance undermined his World Cup chances and he says he does not want to miss out on his chance of carrying Italy's hopes at the European Championships.

"It is one thing to have success in Europe at club level, but another to be successful for your country. The World Cup did not become the opportunity for me that I wanted. I am lucky to have another chance."

And that is irrespective of whom he partners. Most judges are of the view that Vieri and Del Piero do not complement each other well enough. That is good news for Inzaghi who, approaching 27, should be at the height of his powers.

No matter which duo gets the nod – what coach (even Kevin Keegan) wouldn't give his right arm to have Dino Zoff's striking riches!

Inzaghi is a keen student of Italian football history. His big idol was Paolo Rossi, the hero of the 1982 World Cup-winning team. "Rossi was brilliant," he says. "I've seen a lot of him on video and any young striker can learn so much from him. When we won the World Cup he was at his best.

"His anticipation and speed over the first few yards were his biggest weapons. He always seemed to arrive in the right place at the right time. That is not luck. I think all young players would do well to look at pictures of him in action. And I would like to think I have picked up some of his skills from studying him."

And, like Rossi, Inzaghi's eyes are on World Cup glory.

Euro2000 verdict: Italy needs Pippo to pop in the goals.

STATS

Born: 9 August, 1973, Atalanta.

Club: Juventus.

Fee: £9m from Atalanta, June 1997.

QUOTE

"He's a genius around the penalty box."

ALESSANDRO DEL PIERO

DID YOU KNOW?

His younger brother Simone is a striker with Lazio.

19
19

STEFFEN IVERSEN

STRIKER

There was a time when being born a footballer in Norway offered the same chances of fame and fortune as riding a dustcart. But all that has changed. And Steffen Iversen is happy to be around to take full advantage.

His manager at Tottenham, George Graham, is a firm fan of Iversen, an established international who has been a fixture during his country's run to the European finals.

"Steffen has a lot of potential," says Graham. "He is still not the finished article in my view and has been unfortunate with injury both to himself and to his striking partners at Tottenham. Too often he has had to carry the burden up front for us." Graham hasn't been too impressed with the way the Norwegian FA have used Iversen in the past – he returned from the qualifier against Latvia with a heel injury. He was taken off at half-time in that game and missed a few important matches for Spurs, who made an official complaint.

Graham said: "There's a history of lack of communication between Norway and the English clubs who supply their players. We can't do much about it when they have first call on players for World Cup and Euro2000 games but it doesn't encourage you to make them available for friendly games."

Despite such hiccups, Iversen has been happy to commit himself to Tottenham's long-term cause, particularly after enjoying Wembley success in the Worthington Cup last season. Now he wants to go on and achieve a measure of success with Norway who, for a small nation, have a tremendous record in qualifying for major finals.

And Iversen says the Norsemen fancy their chances of coming through their opening group which includes Spain, Yugoslavia and little Slovenia. The Slovenians are familiar opponents, as Norway topped their qualifying group, won 2-1 in Ljubliana and stormed home 4-0 in Oslo in the return match.

Iversen says: "There are no easy matches and Slovenia have improved since we played them, judging by the fact they beat Ukraine in the play-offs. Spain are obviously a form side and Yugoslavia have some very talented players. But we are difficult for sides to score against and have a lot of possibilities to score goals ourselves."

Iversen, signed from Rosenborg in 1996, is favourite to partner Tore-Andre Flo, of Chelsea, in attack, although he has sometimes been used in a deeper role and finds himself under pressure from Norway's new wonder boy, John Carew, for a starting place.

"It is good to have competition for places. The atmosphere in the squad is happy and we have as good a chance as any nation – just look at Denmark in 1992, and the Czechs last time. Neither were among the favourites but had well-balanced sides who all worked for each other."

Now 24, Iversen is an excellent ball player who works tirelessly for his team-mates. His finishing at club level has been criticised in the past, though his strike rate for Norway is good. During qualifying he was often on target during the opening minutes – so defenders will be well warned to watch out for this early bird.

Euro2000 verdict: He could win his Spurs at the finals for Norway.

STATS

Born: 10 November, 1976, Oslo.

Club: Tottenham Hotspur.

Fee: £2.7m from Rosenborg, December 1996.

QUOTE

"Steffen has so much potential."

GEORGE GRAHAM

DID YOU KNOW?

Iversen is an early bird - often scoring quick goals.

HOLSTEN

JENS JEREMIES

MIDFIELDER

Jens Jeremies is probably the closest the Germans have to a genuine replacement for Lothar Matthaus, who is retiring from top-class football after Euro2000. And, in part, it has been Jeremies' disciplinary problems in the last year that have lengthened 39-year-old Matthaus' international career.

The German media pleaded with Matthaus, the most capped player in football history, to postpone his retirement when Jeremies, his Bayern Munich team-mate, picked up a long ban following his Champions' League sending off against PSV Eindhoven.

At least the Germans don't have to go back to Eindhoven for their group clashes with England, Portugal and Romania, so that Jeremies can relive the experience.

Always a tenacious battler, he joined Bayern from local rivals TSV Munich 1860 just after the World Cup. He gives no quarter and was, according to most judges, one of the few German successes of the finals in France, when for once they flopped.

Mind you, a major European poll taken after the finals had the goatee-bearded midfielder-cum-defender in the Nightmare XI – the worst players in the World Cup line-up, with Manchester United's Jaap Stam and Colombia's former Newcastle striker Faustino Asprilla.

That just goes to show how opinion is everything in football. For Bayern chief Franz Beckenbauer believes Jeremies is one of the best German players of his generaton.

"He reminds me a little of Matthaus in his earlier days. He has a presence on the field and does not often give the ball away," says Beckenbauer.

But Jeremies did himself no favours with the PSV incident, and was handed a five-game ban for stamping on an opponent's leg. Both clubs were fined, too, along with PSV coach Eric Gerets. Jeremies is doing his best to put the incident behind him and was a regular starter during Germany's qualifying campaign for Euro2000. He is a very under-rated player, according to Bryan Robson, the Middlesbrough manager.

"Jeremies does a lot of good work for the side and he doesn't always get the praise he should. He sits in front of his defence and races about for the ball which allows people like Stefan Effenberg and Mario Basler to play."

More difficult for Jeremies to live down in the longer term, though, will be the humiliating 3-0 defeat against the United States in a friendly 18 months ago. It left Beckenbauer saying he wished there were more players of Jeremies' calibre coming through the Bundesliga. "For the first time we are finding it hard to produce a new generation," says Beckenbauer.

The German side that day included five Bayern stars: Oliver Kahn, Matthaus, Markus Babbel, Jeremies and Alexander Zickler. "We are a team in change," said Jeremies, "and sometimes you have disappointments like these."

But he knows that not just his coach Erich Ribbeck's head could be on the line if Germany fail to reach the semi-finals at least this summer...

Euro2000 verdict: An important tournament for Jerry & Co.

STATS

Born: 5 March, 1974, Gorlitz, Germany.

Club: Bayern Munich.

Previous club: TSV Munich, July 1998.

QUOTE

'We are a team in change, but we'll bounce back.'

DID YOU KNOW?

He's scored only four league goals since 1994!

adidas
6
6

STEFAN KLOS

GOALKEEPER

It may be a close-run thing, but Stefan Klos hopes to go into Euro2000 for the holders as the man in possession of the No.1 jersey.

Since his transfer to Glasgow Rangers more than a year ago, he has been largely ignored by Germany's coach, Erich Ribbeck, who has sought to find a settled replacement for Bayern's Oliver Kahn.

Kahn is still in Ribbeck's thoughts, but his preferred option for the closing games of the qualifying campaign was Jens Lehmann. "Both are top-class keepers," says Ribbeck, whose team faces England in both the Euro finals opening group and in qualifying for the 2002 World Cup, which begins in the autumn.

Lehmann took over from Klos at Dortmund following his move to Scotland. Ribbeck says: "Stefan is a very good keeper and it is difficult to decide between the three men. Perhaps we should have shirts with 1A 1B and 1C on them!"

Klos, of course, would be thrilled to be part of the German squad and says that competition for places is probably what Germany needs.

And he went to Glasgow with his eyes open. "I knew when I moved to Scotland there was every chance that I would be overlooked at international because Jorg Albertz had warned me that it had happened to him.

"Perhaps if I had gone to the English Premiership it might not have happened but Scottish football has a reputation in Germany. But I still wanted to come to Rangers."

Klos had a hugely successful time at Dortmund under coach Ottmar Hitzfeld, winning the German League crown and the Champions' League, beating Manchester United on the way and Juventus in the final. But he says the move to Rangers came at the right time for him. "It was a fresh challenge and I don't regret it at all."

He has had plenty of opportunity to keep an eye on England's form for the European finals. "The countries have had some battles in the past and I know that there will be plenty of support for me from my Rangers team-mates – especially after England beat Scotland to qualify!

"Scotland were very unlucky at Wembley. They probably deserved a second goal.

"I'm sure it will be close, but there are other dangerous sides in the group – Portugal have a very talented young team who have been together for some time, and Romania will be hard to break down. It is a difficult draw."

He said the Germans should not be unduly worried about England – the Three Lions haven't been rampant against the old enemy since 1966, five years before he was born.

For Klos's part, all he can do is sit and wait to see if he gets the nod over his two major rivals. He has no doubts about his ability if he does. Nor do Rangers fans...

Euro2000 verdict: Could be a Klos call after all...

STATS

Born: August 16, 1971, Dortmund.

Club: Glasgow Rangers.

Fee: £700,000, December 1998.

QUOTE

"Perhaps we should have more keeper's shirts."

ERICH RIBBECK

DID YOU KNOW?

Stefan won the Champions' League with Dortmund in 1997.

PATRICK KLUIVERT

STRIKER

Patrick Kluivert says he is a shy, retiring type of chap, never happier than when he's gone fishing in his homeland. That's quite a contrast to his image and indeed to the hugely controversial path the 23-year-old Dutch striker's career has followed.

Kluivert made his debut for Ajax at 17, scored 18 goals in just 16 starts, including one that won the European Cup and broke into the Dutch international team. Explosive start, or what?

He has since been as likely to hook a controversial headline as a 10lb trout. He left Ajax, looking for bigger fish to fry. In his wake was a conviction for manslaughter following a road accident and an unproven charge of rape. But at Milan he struggled, scoring only six goals in 26 starts and his career was in despair. He was rescued when his former Ajax coach Louis van Gaal signed him for Barcelona.

"In Italy, I was played out of position," Kluivert says. "I prefer to be the centre of three strikers."

The move to Spain breathed new life into Kluivert, who turned down a transfer to Manchester United. And, barring a sending off against Belgium, he had a good World Cup, scoring in the semi-final against Brazil which the Dutch lost on penalties.

"We did quite well and it was a pity we lost the play-off to Croatia because we wanted to finish third after missing out on a place in the final," he says.

The squad was much more united than the one that played in Euro96. Kluivert scored the goal in the 4-1 thrashing by England that saw Holland sneak through the group stage at Scotland's expense.

"The divisions in the camp have been well reported," says Kluivert. "But I think with Frank Rijkaard as coach and everyone fit, we will once more have a united squad. Much more will be expected of us but I think we can deliver."

Kluivert says he prefers his club football to internationals. "The club pays my wages. World Cups and other big events come around less often and only then do I really focus on the Dutch team."

Events in his past have helped shape his outlook. He says the bad times, particularly his brushes with the law, made him think about the friends he was keeping. "There are too many of the fairweather kind. Now I can count my true friends on the fingers of just one hand.

"I have done some things wrong but I have no enduring regrets over those mistakes. I prefer to look forward to better things," he says.

And, no doubt, once Euro2000 is over, that will include a spell down by the river bank. "It's one thing I miss at Barcelona. There is not a lot of good fishing.

"I like to go when I am back in Holland. I love fishing. It is so quiet and it gives me peace of mind," says Kluivert.

But you can be sure he won't be letting too many opposing sides off the hook...

Euro2000 verdict: Big and broody – Kluivert is a defender's worst nightmare...

STATS

Born: 1 July, 1976, Amsterdam.

Club: Barcelona.

Previous clubs: Ajax, AC Milan.

QUOTE

'Much is expected of us – but I think we can deliver.'

DID YOU KNOW?

Patrick scored the European Cup winner in his first season, aged 17.

FRANK LEBOEUF

DEFENDER

World Cup winner Frank Leboeuf is one of football's most colourful characters. The shaven-headed French international defender is outspoken in his views and never far from controversy on the field.

But he says that, having won almost everything in the game, he is close to finally hanging up his boots. He'd like to do so with Chelsea and France both crowned Champions of Europe and says: "After that, what else will there be for me to win, to do?"

Leboeuf was elevated to fame in the World Cup on home soil. He played a starring role in the 3-0 win over Brazil in the final after stepping in for the suspended Laurent Blanc.

"I have won the FA Cup, the Coca-Cola Cup and the European Cup Winners' Cup – and now I am a world champion," he says. "I am so happy. I feel half-English and half-French. My career has taken off since I came to London."

The critics in his native country have never been convinced of his ability – and he has enjoyed proving them all wrong.

Winning the Word Cup was a feeling hard to beat, he recalls: "I felt that 60 million French people were out there with us for the final. They were everywhere, urging us on, willing us to win.

"We were the best side, we did not lose a game, had the best defence, midfield and attack – and beat Brazil 3-0. No-one can take that away from us. It is history and we made it happen – the players and the country together."

Mind you, the man picked on by David Beckham last year as 'Big Ears' says there has been a down side to becoming a champion – he puts down his critics by saying: "It doesn't matter – I won the World Cup".

He admits that made him come across unfairly as arrogant. "Players now want to fight me on the pitch, in the tunnel – and they keep saying I taunted them with my medal. But it's just not true."

Leboeuf, who hit back at Beckham, calling him 'a spoilt child', says his dad was responsible for much of what he has achieved in the game. "My father was my manager when I was young and he devised a training schedule which gave me a good technique and taught me to see situations developing quicker than other players."

He'll need to be at his best when France take on the co-hosts, Holland, in their opening group. But he believes the World Champions can add the European crown to their laurels.

Then it will be off in a cloud of dust, touring the USA on a huge motor-bike.

"I love Harley Davidsons. They are so stylish and they look and sound so good. One day I would love to ride a Harley down Route 66 in America. That's a real retirement dream of mine."

And you sense that day is growing nearer for this popular defender.

Euro2000 verdict: Frank takes no prisoners.

STATS

Born: 22 January, 1968, Marseilles.

Club: Chelsea.

Fee: £2.5m from Strasbourg, July 1996.

QUOTE

"Players say I taunt them with my World Cup medal."

DID YOU KNOW?

Frank's dream is to ride off on a Harley motorcycle.

adidas
4
adidas

OYVIND LEONHARDSEN

MIDFIELDER

George Graham splashed out a lot of money for Norwegian midfielder Oyvind Leonhardsen, expecting him to be a provider of goals. But the former Wimbledon and Liverpool man almost instantly solved a goalscoring crisis at Tottenham.

At one point last season, Leonhardsen was Spurs' leading scorer and contributed with great enthusiasm and effectiveness in place of injured England wide man Darren Anderton.

His renewed goal form, after a season in Liverpool's reserves, brought him back into the fold for Norway, alongside Spurs team-mate Steffen Iversen. Leonhardson, who had been involved in Norway's World Cup efforts, was in the side for their opening Euro2000 qualifier at home to Romania, a 0-0 draw, but was discarded as new coach Nils Johan Semb assembled his thoughts after succeeding Egil Olsen.

Leonhardsen was a tremendous fan of Olsen, now manager of Wimbledon, though the pair never worked together at Selhurst Park as Leonhardsen had by then moved to Liverpool, joining the Anfield club in a £3.5m deal in 1997.

Leonhardsen says: "Egil is a great manager. He makes you believe in your ability and for me he is the best manager I ever worked for. I'm sure he is the right man for the job at Wimbledon, as long as he is given time.

"He made me an international player and I will always be grateful for that."

Norway did remarkably well after a stumbling start which left them with only one point from their first two qualifying games. They turned things round with a 2-1 win in Slovenia, with whom they are paired again in Holland and Belgium this summer.

By then, though, Leonhardsen was not involved to any major degree, though he was recalled for a friendly in May 1999 against the Reggae Boys, Jamaica, which Norway won 6-0. He was on the scoresheet and was retained for the crucial home win over Georgia ten days later.

He scored the only goal against Greece last September and was on target again, along with Iversen, in the 4-0 hammering of Slovenia in Oslo that booked the Norwegians' place in the finals.

"Steffen and I have worked well together since I joined Tottenham. That has helped us at international level, too. We have a good understanding of each other's runs."

Leonhardsen is a tireless worker, getting up and down the pitch. His manager at Wimbledon, Joe Kinnear, used to say he had a good engine. But Kinnear was quick to recognise the player's ball skills, particularly his ability to cross and pass accurately.

"Oyvind was a useful provider of goals for us. He'd offer himself as an outlet when we got forward, and he was quick to react when moves broke down. He was a real asset to us," said Kinnear. He believes Leonhardsen is the ideal player for teams that play positive, direct football. And Norway certainly do that, though less so since Olsen took that brand to Wimbledon.

Euro2000 verdict: Leo is Norway's natural star sign!

STATS

Born: 17 August, 1970, Kristiansund.

Club: Tottenham.

Fee: £3m from Liverpool, August, 1999.

QUOTE

"Egil Olsen made me an international player."

DID YOU KNOW?

He's won more than 65 caps for his country.

UMBRO
8

BIXENTE LIZARAZU

DEFENDER

In the red corner, weighing in at... well, a lot less than his opponent, the flying French wingback. I give you... World Cup-winning Bayern Munich star Bixente Lizarazu.

It might not have been the Fight of the Century, but the pint-sized Lizarazu's much-publicised training-ground fight with German team-mate Lothar Matthaus last year earned almost as many headlines as a Lennox Lewis title bout.

Lizarazu ended £5,000 down – but it was not because he lost the contest, indeed he gave as good as he got. That was the fine imposed by Bayern chiefs afterwards.

Fortunately both France and Germany are seeded well apart in the Euro2000 finals. But the brilliant little former Bordeaux wing-back whose performances in the last World Cup won him rave reviews, says the Matthaus incident was over-hyped.

"Being in the newspapers is typical of Bayern," he says. "Sometimes there are troubles but the press like these things for their headlines. Little things become big problems, just because it's Bayern.

"About Lothar – since I've been at the club he has played very well for Bayern. We did have a problem together. But that is over now."

Once the squabble was resolved it seemed Bayern put their early-season troubles behind them last term. They stemmed from their Champions' League final defeat against Manchester United. "After that disappointment, it was difficult to motivate ourselves. And the same was true for many of the French team that won the World Cup. It was a huge achievement and, for many of us, it left us drained of emotion and physical strength for quite a time.

"It didn't affect me as much, though losing to Manchester United hurt a lot, especially when it seemed we had the game won."

Lizarazu will be an important part of Roger Lemerre's team, drawn in the opening phase with Holland, the dangerous Czechs and Denmark. "This looks to be the most difficult group," he says. "We must be on top form from the first moment of the first match.

"But the World Cup also taught us much about playing these big tournaments and I think that will help us."

This time there will be none of the burden of expectation of being hosts, and Lizarazu believes that could be a big factor when France play Holland, in their final group game, in Amsterdam. "There could be so much depending on that result, and the pressure on them could help us," says Lizarazu.

A stylish operator with a shrewd football brain, it was the pace and quality of Lizarazu's passing that impressed everyone in the World Cup. And England fans have twice seen him stifle the effectiveness of David Beckham, most recently when the French won a friendly at Wembley in February 1999 – their first at the famous stadium.

Lizarazu performed the same task well in that epic Champions' League final, containing Beckham and his famed crosses. Now he's aiming to add the European crown to his World Cup medal – and if he does, he'll be punching the air, not a team-mate, he promises!

Euro2000 verdict: Pocket-sized performer with a big reputation.

STATS

Born: 9 December, 1969, France.

Club: Bayern Munich, joined July 1997.

Previous club: Bordeaux.

QUOTE

"Our key match will come against Holland."

DID YOU KNOW?

He played against Bayern in the 1996 UEFA Cup final.

3
adidas

FREDDIE LJUNGBERG

MIDFIELD

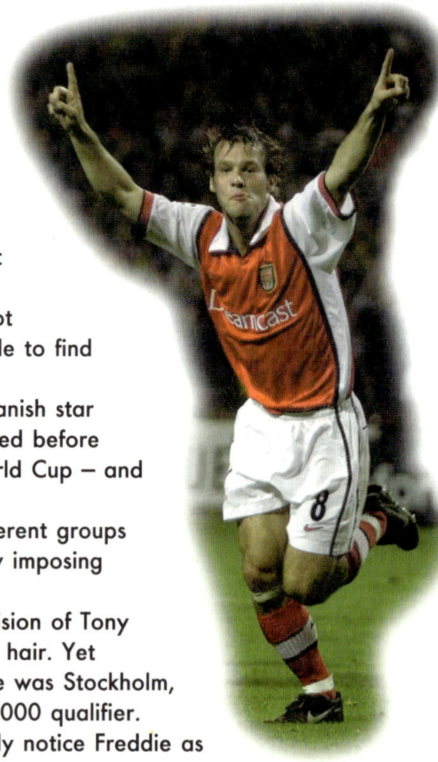

The quiet Swedish seaside resort of Halmstad's best-known export was pop duo Roxette – until Freddie Ljungberg, the man with the colourful punk-rocker hairstyle, moved to Arsenal for £3m and became an instant hit.

Ljungberg scored on his Gunners debut – against Manchester United, no less. He had come off the bench to replace French striker Nicolas Anelka. And, in scoring after just four minutes 42 seconds, he became the fastest Gunner of all time to claim his first goal for the club.

That left even Ian Wright in his wake. And for Sid Ljungberg, as he is known at Highbury because of his punk look in the mould of Sid Vicious, that goal cemented an amazing rise to prominence.

Halmstad are only a part-time club, and Ljungberg spent his time, when not doing extra training, at Tylosand, a beach resort in Sweden. "It was incredible to find myself playing in the Premiership and scoring so soon after that," he recalls.

One man who didn't share in the delight was United's keeper that day, Danish star Peter Schmeichel. For, as Ljungberg remembers: "One of the last goals I scored before joining Arsenal was for Sweden against Denmark, shortly before the last World Cup – and that one beat Schmeichel, too!"

Fortunately for Schmeichel, Sweden and Denmark have been drawn in different groups in the Euro finals. Ljungberg is pleased about that, too, though: "He is a very imposing person when he comes out of goal at you."

Ljungberg's only memory of the goal celebration against United was the vision of Tony Adams patting him on the head and saying something about the spikes in his hair. Yet Adams was hard-pressed to remember when the pair had last met. The venue was Stockholm, when England were led a merry dance by the Swedes in their opening Euro2000 qualifier.

"I was so wrapped up in my own job in the international that I didn't really notice Freddie as an individual," says Adams. "But I know there were Swedish players causing us problems on their left – they turned out to be Freddie and my old Arsenal team-mate Stefan Schwarz." Ljungberg and Schwarz room together on international duty and Schwarz was able to give his team-mate the inside track on life at Highbury.

Ljungberg takes after Ian Wright in that he is prone to getting into trouble on the pitch with his aggressive approach. He admits: "My temper is like Wright's and has got me into trouble before." He got into strife in the North London derby with Tottenham last season, when he made a V-sign to fans after being sent off somewhat harshly at White Hart Lane.

In a stroke he wiped out much of the credit he had got when Sweden's win against Poland helped England to qualify for the European finals.

"Tony Adams and David Seaman were among the first to congratulate me after the Poland match and I was pleased that England qualified for the finals. I think they could be a big danger," he says.

As for Sweden, they need more goals from Ljungberg and Co. if they are to be serious title contenders, though Ljungberg says: "I think we'll be one of the toughest teams to beat."

Euro2000 verdict: Ready, Freddie, Go...

STATS

Born: 16 April, 1977, Sweden.

Club: Arsenal.

Fee: £3m from Halmstad, September 1998.

QUOTE

" My temper is a bit like Ian Wright's! "

DID YOU KNOW?

Freddie scored on his Arsenal debut against Man United.

adidas
ULTIMAX

STEVE McMANAMAN

MIDFIELDER

Steve McManaman had a harsh send-off when he left Liverpool for the Spanish giants Real Madrid a year ago. He was accused of only going for the money, and that he had not pulled his weight for Liverpool – or for his country.

But Macca is adamant that money was only secondary. In his heart he'll always be a Liverpudlian, and he swells with pride every time he wears the Three Lions of England.

"I had to put up with people saying I was concentrating on my move to Madrid instead of the Liverpool cause. But that was untrue," said McManaman. "My appearance record for Liverpool was fantastic, barring injuries. I missed only a handful of games in my time at Anfield, except when I had a serious achilles injury and then another bad one after a tackle.

"The manager would say that in my last months with Liverpool I was getting better and better. It's just that results weren't happening for the club."

He was disappointed not to gain anything like the awards of the Reds during the heyday of Kevin Keegan, now the England coach. Sadly for Keegan, the timing of McManaman's injuries left him unable to call on the player who was a star of Euro96, when Terry Venables gave him the freedom to run at defences.

There is no doubt that McManaman is naturally gifted. And he's equipped with nimbleness and raw pace – priceless assets in today's game. Yet too often for club and country, Macca has been strait-jacketed on the wing.

Time will tell, but it seems McManaman is destined to bear the burden once carried by John Barnes, another former Anfield great, who seldom produced his best football at international level.

Perhaps it was a positional thing, or the fact that McManaman is not cut out for defensive duties. The player himself says: "I'm happy on either side of the park – anywhere as long as I'm in the team!" The move to Spain was part of what McManaman – a columnist in *The Times* – says is his continuing football education. At first it was a sort of home from home, with Keegan's former partner in goals, John Toshack, there as coach.

But Macca also knew he would get no favours from Toshack, who was later sacked after a poor run of results in the Spanish Primera Liga. He had to fight for his place alongside the likes of the brilliant Dutchman Clarence Seedorf and the fiery Argentinian, Fernando Redondo. But McManaman says: "That's all part of the challenge."

He says football is more tactical in Spain, which perhaps is why so few Englishman succeed over there. "It's a battle of wits, and I think English players mostly prefer the fast pace of the Premiership."

A fit McManaman – one who has had a decent run of games in the multi-cultural Spanish League – will be a huge asset for Keegan. But he can also use Macca in another enormously helpful way. As a spy. With many of Europe's star names in action each week in Spain, McManaman can give Keegan briefings on some of England's Euro 2000 opponents.

Above all, England's midfield has been without that touch of individual flair and imagination. McManaman, back in harness with his old Liverpool mates Michael Owen and Robbie Fowler, could be the man to provide it.

Euro2000 verdict: Macca can – if Keegan gives him license to thrill.

STATS

Born: 11 February, 1972, Liverpool.

Club: Real Madrid.

Fee: Free from Liverpool, 1999.

QUOTE

'I'm happy playing anywhere – as long as I'm in the team!'

DID YOU KNOW?

He signed for Liverpool at 11 – but was an Everton fan.

11
11

PAOLO MALDINI

DEFENDER

Not so long ago, Paolo Maldini was widely heralded as the world's best defender. No money could prise him away from AC Milan, where he is both captain and spiritual leader.

And it is not so much that he has declined in recent seasons – more that Milan has lost its gloss and the invincibility of the 1980s, when the San Siro club ruled Europe and Maldini quickly stamped his mark on the side.

He is the son of Cesare Maldini, a former AC Milan defender and the man who led Italy at the last World Cup. Young Paolo didn't take long to emerge from his father's shadow and indeed might even emulate his achievements as a coach once he retires from playing.

Maldini was 16 when he made his Milan debut in 1985 against Udinese. Before long he was also in Italy's Under-21 side, coached at the time by his dad. And at 19 he'd made the step up to the full international team, taking part in the European Championship finals in Germany. He was the youngest player to take part in the tournament.

His model looks and unflappable temperament have made him a huge draw away from football. He has taken to the catwalk in his favourite Versace suits and has modelled for Nike, car makers Opel, and De Rigo, the makers of police sunglasses.

One of six children, he has never really had it tough. Some have unkindly said that his dad opened doors for him – but his talent makes a lie of that.

A cultured left back who has also been known to score goals, he has won almost every honour at club level. That includes five Serie A titles, three Champions Club Cups, three European Super Cups and two Intercontinental Cups with Milan.

At international level, however, such success has eluded him. The closest he has come to the biggest prize in the game was the 1994 World Cup Final defeat by Brazil in a penalty shoot-out, though he was equally upset at Italy's failure not to lift the trophy on home soil four years earlier.

"He's a fantastic defender. Technically very gifted," says Chelsea manager Gianluca Vialli, who would love to lure him to Stamford Bridge.

Maldini may well try once more for World Cup glory – with Euro2000 a major stepping-stone along the way – before trying his luck in the USA, a country he loves with a passion. "I'd love to live in New York," he says.

And beyond that? He's not sure, but who knows, with a young son, Christian, by his Italian-Venezuelan model wife Adriana Fossa, we could yet see another Maldini in the blue shirt of Italy before too long...

Euro2000 verdict: All wannabe defenders should watch this one in action.

STATS

Born: 26 June, 1968, Milan.

Club: AC Milan.

Fee: None. AC Milan junior.

QUOTE

"He's a fantastic defender. Very gifted."

GIANLUCA VIALLI

DID YOU KNOW?

His dad was Italy's coach at the World Cup.

ITALIA
3

LOTHAR MATTHAUS

DEFENDER

For enduring success, Lothar Matthaus has no equal in modern football. Besides being the most capped player in the history of the game, few have won more prizes than the Bayern Munich star.

Indeed, Matthaus overhauled the world record number of caps for a footballer, 143, as the Germans qualified for the finals, beating the record set in 1997 by Swedish keeper Thomas Ravelli.

Matthaus, now 39, delayed his retirement, planned for this spring, in order to feature in one last major tournament, Euro2000. After the finals he will be playing for New York Metro Stars in America's Major Soccer League.

Incredibly, it will be 20 years since Matthaus first figured in the European Championships. In 1980 he was still finding his way in the game, but sufficiently admired to be a substitute in West Germany's final success against Belgium.

For many players, captaining your country to victory in the World Cup and being voted player of the tournament would be satisfying enough to begin plans for a quiet retirement. Not so, Matthaus. He reached that pinnacle in 1990 in Italy.

Last season, having long since retired from international football and handed the captain's armband over to Jurgen Klinsmann, Matthaus returned to the big time. He was a major contributor to Germany's qualification for the European finals and deeply involved in Bayern Munich's bid for Champions' League glory after their shock late defeat by Manchester United in 1999.

Matthaus is a magnificent athlete and a model professional. He has looked after himself wonderfully well in a career that has taken him from Borussia Münchengladbach to Bayern Munich, on to Inter Milan for £2.2m in 1988, and back to Bayern, with whom he has since won the UEFA Cup in 1996 and two more Bundesliga titles.

He established himself in the German side at the 1986 World Cup in Mexico, scoring a superb solo goal against Morocco. Whether in midfield or, latterly, as sweeper, Matthaus has always led by example.

The European championship is a prize that, like the Champions' League, has eluded him. He remained on the bench in 1980 and injury robbed him of a chance to pick up winner's medals in 1992 and at Euro96.

Matthaus retired from the international scene after winning his 122nd cap in a 2-1 win over Albania in 1994. But he was talked back into action after former Spurs star Klinsmann hung up his boots, and after injury to Matthias Sammer.

The pair were never the greatest friends and their rivalry spilled over a few years back when it was discovered that Matthaus had bet against Klinsmann scoring 15 goals in a season for Bayern.

Matthaus lost the bet, but when it became public in his book, *Secret Football Diaries*, it needed Bayern president Franz Beckenbauer, formerly Germany's most capped star, to intervene.

He temporarily stripped Matthaus of the Bayern captaincy but then, in true diplomatic fashion, got Matthaus to extend his career to help the club's efforts to rule Europe again.

This, then, will be Matthaus' final outing for his country – and the worry for Germany is the lack of new talent lining up to take his place. What a star... they'll certainly miss him.

Euro2000 verdict: May not have the legs to last the pace, but he has the shrewdest football brain.

STATS

Born: 21 March, 1961, Erlangen.

Club: Bayern Munich.

Previous clubs: B. Münchengladbach, Inter Milan.

QUOTE

'Magnificent athlete and a model professional.'

DID YOU KNOW?

Matthaus is the most capped player in history.

PEDRAG MIJATOVIC

STRIKER

Pedrag Mijatovic will dedicate Yugoslavia's victory to the suffering of his family and many of his fellow countrymen and women if he and his talented team-mates win Euro2000.

It would be a controversial success, for many still believe the Yugoslavs should not be taking part in the competition after the war in the Balkans, over Kosovo, which left many dead, made many more homeless, and disrupted the qualifying competition.

NATO planes bombed Yugoslavia during the height of the troubles and many of the Yugoslav national team's foreign-based stars had to go to great lengths to ensure the safety of their families back home.

Lazio's Serb sweeper Sinisa Mihailovic managed to sneak into neighbouring Hungary just hours before the border was closed. Mijatovic, who was playing in Spain for Real Madrid, recalls: "I came out of Yugoslavia because of my son. If it wasn't for him, I'd have stayed with my parents, who didn't want to leave their house. It was a very sad situation."

Other team-mates had relatives close to Belgrade, which was bombed by NATO planes, and the players united in calls for a quick end to the troubles.

Mijatovic has tried hard to concentrate on his football. The man who scored the winner for Real Madrid in the 1998 Champions' League final against Juventus, moved last year to Italian club Fiorentina, for £6m, to play alongside the Argentinian goal genius Gabriel Batistuta and Italy's striker Enrico Chiesa. All three played in the Champions' League against Arsenal for whom Mijatovic's former Real Madrid strike partner now plays.

Mijatovic, a key figure in Yugoslavia's qualifying run to Euro2000, missed the later clashes with Manchester United owing to a heel injury. It needed an operation that kept him sidelined until the latter part of last season – so he should be fresh for the finals this summer.

Mijatovic has become a folk hero in Florence, where Fiorentina play, with posters to him and his team-mates plastered over the city. He was just as popular in Madrid – and has not been forgotten back home. The national coach, Vujadin Boskov, says Mijatovic is a crucial member of the team.

He says: "We need Pedrag to be fit. He is an important player for Yugoslavia, one of the best strikers in Europe.

"He was unable to play any football, not to kick a ball, for three months. That could take the edge off a player. But I know he is a great player he will be with us in time for the tournament."

Mijatovic's strength is his ability to turn and get a shot at target before defenders have time to react. He may not be the quickest over ten yards, but over half a yard he is lethal. He has worked very well with Batistuta, showing his unselfish attitude in providing goals for 'Batigol' rather than being the focus of the attack himself.

His goal against Juventus two years ago was typical – a loose ball in the box, and he was quickest to react to lift it over the keeper. He doesn't miss much in the six-yard box.

Euro2000 verdict: Slav on a mission – watch this one closely!

STATS

Born: 19 January, 1969, Podgorika, Serbia.

Club: Fiorentina.

Fee: £6m fom Real Madrid, June 1999.

QUOTE

'We need Pedrag to be fully fit.'

VUJADIN BOSKOV

DID YOU KNOW?

His goal won the 1998 Champions' League final for Real Madrid.

8

SAVO MILOSEVIC

STRIKER

Yugoslavia's star striker Savo Milosevic has done much to put behind him the controversy of his departure from Aston Villa. The Serb admits that it was all down to him.

Milosevic outraged Villa fans by spitting at them during a game at Blackburn and refusing to apologise publicly when ordered by the Midland club's manager, John Gregory.

The saga ended with Milosevic being sold to Real Zaragoza, of Spain. Milosevic admitted on Spanish TV: "Everything was great at Villa. I had no problems until this one incident. It ruined everything.

"We were losing at Blackburn and were playing poorly. I missed a chance I should have put away. The fans had been on my back and when they started shouting at me and shaking their fists, I spat at them.

"I lost it in the heat of the moment and I paid the price. I can't blame them or the manager. It was a crazy, crazy thing to do and there was no way I could carry on at Villa after that."

Milosevic has been a huge hit in Spain, averaging virtually a goal a game at Zaragoza, of whom he says: "I owe them so much. They rescued my career." Now Italian club Roma are said to be interested in paying £16m to sign him and to treble his salary. That must have broken Gregory's heart as Villa struggled for goals. For the 26-year-old former Partizan Belgrade striker, who scored in their League Cup final triumph against Leeds three years ago, cost Villa £3.6m. Former boss Brian Little had never seen him play in the flesh before securing the deal on the strength of a few videos.

Savo had mixed fortunes at Villa Park. Villa fans admired his bravery and his ability to pop in goals from all angles. But they did have doubts about his temperament. It can't have been easy for Milosevic too settle, though, given the strife in his homeland. He admitted he often had fears for the safety of his family.

But he has put the past behind him by concentrating on his football and using all his strengths in the Spanish Primera Liga. He is a strong character, athletically built and with decent awareness of half a chance. His current goals ratio shows he will be a big threat in Holland and Belgium this summer. Milosevic is flattered by the interest from Roma but says he owes Zaragoza so much and will show them that when he sits down to thrash out a new contract with them.

Matters should be resolved by the time the Euro2000 finals kick off. The left-footed striker will be used as a target man for his country, with Predraj Mijatovic spinning off him and Dejan Savicevic operating just behind.

Yugoslavia have been drawn with Spain, so there will be much interest in that game, given Milosevic's presence for the Slavs. The teams meet in Bruges on June 21 and the pressure could be on either or both sides to get a result that evening. "I hope we both go through to the next round," says Milosevic. "Otherwise it might be tough for me to return to Zaragoza if we've knocked Spain out of the tournament!"

Euro2000 verdict: Savo's no longer the Villain!

STATS

Born: 2 September, 1973, Bijeljuna.

Club: Real Zaragoza.

Fee: £3.5m from Aston Villa, March 1998.

QUOTE

'It was crazy how it fell apart for me at Villa. But it was all my fault.'

DID YOU KNOW?

Savo was Villa's £3.5m record signing from Partizan Belgrade.

adidas
18

FERNANDO MORIENTES
STRIKER

Spain's Fernando Morientes had the perfect start to his international career, scoring twice in the first five minutes in a 4-0 friendly win against Sweden. If only it were always that simple!

The Real Madrid striker knows from his time at the Bernabeu Stadium that sometimes things go your way and sometimes they don't. You just have to take every chance that comes along.

Morientes and Real team-mate Raul have struck up a superb partnership. But it has not always been a first-choice one for Madrid. Especially since the arrival of Liverpool's Steve McManaman and £23m long-time misfit Frenchman Nicolas Anelka.

Had he not been such a bitter rival for a place in the Real starting side, Morientes might have felt a great deal of sympathy for Anelka's problems at the club. In particular his failure to find the net until the FIFA Club World Championship in Brazil, where it suddenly all began to click – the penalty miss and injury aside.

Anelka did himself few favours during his pre-Christmas goal drought by claiming that Morientes and Raul were making life tough for him by refusing to pass to him – overtones of Bergkamp and Overmars during the moody teenager's time at Arsenal.

Morientes is a laid-back character with a superb temperament on the field. And a wise head for one so young. In come the new stars, with the aim of either displacing you or making you reach new peaks to hold your place in the side.

The youthful-looking Morientes – he's 24 – had put the senior men under pressure himself when he arrived in the Real first team.

Then, the men in possession were Croatian striker Davor Suker – top scorer at the last World Cup – and Yugoslavian Predraj Mijatovic.

So, when Lorenzo Sanz, the Real president enthused about Anelka being 'one of the five best players in the world' and that Real 'needed a signing like this to complete our team – next stop Champions' League and Spanish League glory', Morientes knew he had little to lose. The pressure would be on Anelka. And it showed.

The player also knows that Real's notorious Ultrasur fans didn't much like Anelka from the start – the local boy was always going to be their favourite. Morientes' greater worry all along was that anything less than regular games for Real would cost him his place in Spain's side.

Spain wiped out all opposition during qualifying, scoring a staggering 45 goals in eight games – that included losing their opening tie, a 3-2 shocker in Cyprus.

Raul and Morientes got Spain's goals that day and the latter was on target again when Jose Antonio Camacho's men signed off their campaign with a 3-0 win over Israel. Between times, Morientes was less involved as Camacho widened his franchise to beyond the usual group of Real and Barcelona players.

But Morientes kept up his form, scoring freely in the Madrid side's Champions' League campaign.

He's sure to be involved as Spain look to build on their magnificent qualifying form when they open against Norway in Rotterdam on June 13.

Euro2000 verdict: Fernando's the Real deal.

STATS

Born: 5 April, 1976, Spain.

Club: Real Madrid, joined July 1997.

Previous club: Real Zaragoza.

QUOTE

'He has a superb partnership with team-mate Raul.'

DID YOU KNOW?

Fernando scored 28 goals in 68 games for Zaragoza.

9

PAVEL NEDVED

MIDFIELDER

Brilliant Lazio midfielder Pavel Nedved will play a crucial role as the Czech Republic try to go one better this summer than their Euro96 final defeat against Germany.

Nedved is the typical Czech international of the modern game – he plays his football abroad. Indeed, coach Josef Chovanec had just three home-based players in his squad when the Czechs played their qualifying game in Scotland. That would have been unheard of years ago, when the Czech authorities refused visas for players to go abroad.

When the barriers came down, Nedved was one of the most sought-after players on the shopping list of Italian clubs.

But the Czech footballing public, denied seeing their stars on home grounds, refuse to desert the heroes who have deserted them. Nedved is as popular as tennis stars Ivan Lendl and Martina Navratilova, who also sought their fortune on foreign shores.

Nedved, a key figure for the most exciting team in Italy last term, the Rome club Lazio, may not even be there next season, if recent reports are to be believed, with Juventus expected to table an amazing £15m bid to make him Zinedine Zidane's replacement. Nedved scored Lazio's winner in the Cup-Winners' Cup final against Real Mallorca at Aston Villa last year. The only thing that has tested his fans' patience back home is Nedved's recent decision to apply for Italian citizenship. The Czech press pilloried Nedved for a time, though the initial fury has since died down and he'll be able to shine up his reputation as his country's golden boy with victory this summer in the Low Countries.

They were in magnificent form in the qualifiers, and Nedved scored twice in a superb display in Lithuania, where the Czechs won 4-0. He helped set up Jan Koller's pair of goals, too. Injury kept him out of their final two qualifying matches but by then the Czechs had all but qualified and went on to win ten out of ten.

"We were brilliant at times during those matches," says Nedved. "I just hope we can carry that form into the finals."

He believes the Czechs have the toughest draw, paired with Holland, world champions France and Denmark. "But our record has been very good, we have some very talented players, and I think other teams will treat us with a lot of respect."

Nedved has learned much from his time in Italy and having the Argentinian hard-men Diego Simeone and Juan Veron alongside frees him to be at his most creative, providing the bullets for Chilean striker Marcelo Salas and the prolific Simone Inzaghi, brother of Juventus's Pippo Inzaghi.

Another team-mate, Sweden's Kennet Andersson, Nedved rates very highly and says the Swedes could be the dark horses of the tournament, just as the Czechs were four years ago. "They have some very good players and qualified strongly. They will be difficult to score goals against and could even finish ahead of Italy in that section."

Euro2000 verdict: The Czechs' key player needs his best Lazio form.

STATS

Born: 30 August, 1972, Cheb, Czech Republic.

Club: Lazio.

Previous clubs: Dukla Prague, Sporta Prague.

QUOTE

"Teams will treat us with more respect now."

DID YOU KNOW?

Juventus are set to bid £15m for Pavel.

ALLAN NIELSEN

MIDFIELDER

Allan Nielsen goes to Euro2000 with his club future under a cloud. The man whose goal won the Worthington Cup for Tottenham in 1999 is said to be a transfer target of Middlesbrough after his growing disenchantment at being left on the bench too often.

He has been worried that his lack of regular first-team exposure is a threat to his chances of starting for Denmark in their opening clash with France in Bruges on June 11.

The midfielder joined Spurs for £1.65m from Danish champions Brondby after beginning his career with hometown club Esbjerg. He had spells with Bayern Munich, Syon, Odense and FC Copenhagen.

But now it could be time to pack his bags again and Spurs fans will be sad to see him go. An honest battler, Nielsen has the knack of scoring vital goals. In 1998-99 he bagged just nine – but they included a League Cup strike in the win over Liverpool, and, of course, his header in injury-time that broke Leicester's hearts in the Wembley final.

But the arrival of Steffen Freund and Tim Sherwood has limited his opportunities, and he has already had one written transfer request thrown out last summer. George Graham will be tempted to let Nielsen go if a club matches his £4m valuation.

Nielsen says: "It hurts to be left out of any side and I want to play every game. I am happy at Spurs but I'm 28 now and I have to be playing first-team football. I don't feel I have anything left to prove. The manager knows what I can bring to the team."

Matters weren't helped at the start of last season when Nielsen suffered a freak injury before the pre-season game with Hearts, when he damaged a hamstring in the warm-up.

But whatever strife he faces at club level, Nielsen can take some heart that he is still in favour with Denmark, even after a change of manager.

He scored a crucial goal in the 2-1 home defeat of Switzerland in qualifying, and starred in Denmark's shock 3-2 win in Italy, who topped Group 1 by just a point. Denmark had trailed 2-0 in that one and looked on their way out of the tournament.

The Danes had to face Israel over two legs in the play-offs after edging out the Swiss on goal difference. But the Israelis were no match, losing 8-0 on aggregate.

"The way we qualified was amazing," says Nielsen. "It was a fairytale. To win our last four matches after losing two and drawing two shows the spirit in the side.

"It shows we can go to the finals and not fear anyone. And why can't we win it? No-one gave us much chance in 1992 but we won. The spirit is much as it was then," he adds.

Euro2000 verdict: One-Niel to the Denmark.

STATS

Born: 13 March, 1971, Esbjerg, Denmark.

Club: Tottenham Hotspur.

Fee: £1.65m from Brondby, September 1996.

QUOTE

"To qualify after our poor start was a fairytale."

DID YOU KNOW?

Allan scored Spurs' Wembley winner in the Worthington Cup.

hummel
7
DBU

MARC OVERMARS

MIDFIELDER

When Holland open their Euro2000 finals campaign in Amsterdam, you might not notice the advertising hoardings around the edge of the pitch. But you can be sure Marc Overmars will be keeping one eye open for them after a collision with one in the Olympic Stadium a few years back almost ended his career.

Arsenal's flying Dutchman was playing for Ajax against De Grafschaap in a league match when he was pushed by an opponent, lost his footing on the edge of the turf and careered into the hoardings. He severely damaged his knee ligaments. It is the sort of injury that so often finishes players, or reduces them to a shadow of their former selves, robbing them of that extra yard of pace. Paul Gascoigne, who suffered a similar injury in the 1991 FA Cup Final for Tottenham, was never quite the same again.

But while many feared for Overmars, whose blistering pace is his greatest weapon, the player himself, then just 22, was concerned only at the amount of hard work he faced, trying to recapture his fitness.

And he proved the doubters wrong when he started clocking times in sprints that were the equal of his pre-injury days. The injury did, however, cost him a place in the Dutch squad for Euro96 in England. It wasn't all bad, though, for Holland were poor – and got hammered 4-1 by England at Wembley.

He went quietly about his business and Arsenal were quick off the mark to sign him for more than £5m in the summer of 1997.

Overmars had won the Champions' League with Ajax. His first season in England was crowned with a Premiership and FA Cup Double for the Gunners. And he then went on to star in the World Cup finals in France.

He had such a good World Cup 98 that many judges reckon that his unfortunate hamstring injury during the later stages possibly cost the Dutch a place in the final at the expense of Brazil.

Overmars was restricted to just 30 minutes of the quarter-final against Argentina, famed for his Gunners team-mate Dennis Bergkamp's brilliant late winner. And Overmars could only watch the following match against Brazil, which Ronaldo and Co. won to earn a showdown with the hosts, France.

Guus Hiddink, then the Dutch coach, said: "If Marc had been fit, I think he could have been the difference for us. His pace is electrifying and his finishing is reliable when he gets a chance at goal."

Overmars says: "I don't think we'll get another chance like that to win a World Cup, so it is a painful memory for me. But playing the European Championships on home soil will be wonderful. The Dutch people were so excited by our performances in France.

"It will bring some pressure, because we will be expected to do well and our results in recent times have not been so good. But you have to believe in yourselves to win major tournaments and we have so many good players these days.

"I know that in football you don't only have good times. My injury taught me that. But I think we have a very good chance of winning Euro2000, and that would make up for some of the unfortunate things that have happened in the past."

Euro2000 verdict: Holland will be over the moon if Overmars is fully fit.

STATS

Born: 29 March, 1973, Emst, Holland.

Club: Arsenal.

Fee: £5m from Ajax, 1997.

QUOTE

"A fit Overmars could have won us the World Cup."

GUUS HIDDINK

DID YOU KNOW?

He was injured and missed the Euro96 defeat by England.

KNVB
14
14

MICHAEL OWEN

STRIKER

England's boy wonder is going to find the going tough at the European Championships. The critics make much of his greatest asset, his pace. But the teenage Liverpool striker lost an even bigger weapon – surprise – in France two years ago, when he scored one of the great World Cup goals.

That solo strike against Argentina removed for ever his cloak of mystery and in one moment made him one of the game's hottest properties.

In truth, Owen is still a long way from the finished article, and doubts over whether he can work effectively alongside Alan Shearer remain. In England's play-off ties with Scotland the young Scouser was a shadow of his brilliant best, too often giving up possession or trying to be too fancy after beating one defender.

But there is no doubt that he is the best of his generation. Ruud Gullit, the former Newcastle United manager, says: "Michael has an awareness, a football intellect far beyond his years."

And Gullit's successor at St James' Park, former England manager Bobby Robson, adds: "The kid's pace is frightening. I don't care how good a defender you are, his pace would give you nightmares. And his finishing is nerveless."

People have been saying such things since Owen was a schoolboy, not that long ago, of course. Apart from a couple of years at the FA School of Excellence at Lilleshall, Owen lived his life in Wales and attended Welsh schools.

Since he was eight, he was always the best player in every team in which he played – by a long way. Manchester United wanted to sign him on the spot when Sir Alex Ferguson's former assistant, Brian Kidd, watched him score all six goals for Deeside Schools when he was 11. But he lived too far from the club and, after spending a couple of weeks at Old Trafford as a teenager, he joined Liverpool. And that is despite being a fan of Everton.

His big idol was always Gary Lineker. Owen was too young to remember him star for England in the 1986 World Cup, but is hugely proud of wearing his old No. 10 shirt.

And, while he's shy to admit it, Owen would love to be as successful as Lineker for his country. It was in the 1992 European Championships in Sweden that Lineker signed off his international career with 47 goals – one short of the all-time record held by Sir Bobby Charlton.

Only time will tell whether Owen has what it takes to become part of such an exclusive club. "I know I still have a lot to learn," he says. "I always try to profit from things that don't go right in matches. And there are always plenty of people to pick you up on your mistakes!"

Injury stopped him being a major contributor to England's cause in qualifying for the European finals. But a fully-fit Michael Owen, maturing with every match, is sure to be one of Kevin Keegan's biggest assets this summer.

The only major worry is his temperament – he is prone to having a short fuse. If he can channel his aggression, he'll be the perfect player.

Euro2000 verdict: He could make these Championships his Owen!

STATS

Born: 14 December, 1979, Chester.

Club: Liverpool.

Fee: None. Liverpool juniors.

QUOTE

"The kid's pace is frightening."

BOBBY ROBSON

DID YOU KNOW?

He's the youngest player to wear a full England shirt.

ENGLAND
18
18

EMMANUEL PETIT

MIDFIELDER

Manu Petit is not the sort of person to let doubt get the better of him. However, the pony-tailed Arsenal midfield maestro must have been a bit alarmed when so much came his way in 1998.

How do you ever live up to winning a League and Cup Double? Oh, and a World Cup? Yeah, and you score one of the goals in the final... against Brazil.

It can't get any better, can it? Possibly not, unless you count leaving the post-World Cup banquet, sticking your last few Francs in a fruit machine and needing a bucket to collect the winnings. You guessed it – that happened, too. Petit picked up a cool £17,000.

Since then, though, Petit has been struggling to find the same pitch in terms of motivation and performance. Injuries have not helped, but the Dieppe-born 29-year-old, who joined the Gunners from Monaco for £3.5m a few years back, has been a shadow of his immaculate best. He did not figure very much in the Euro2000 qualifying competition.

Mind you, neither did Zinedine Zidane. Take those two out of the side and you can see why France looked anything like World champions as they sneaked into the finals with a late goal against Iceland.

Petit has been the cornerstone of Wenger's French revolution at Highbury. His partnership with Patrick Vieira has been the envy of the Premiership. But injuries and disciplinary problems have reduced their number of starts in the same team, and consequently affected their chances of recreating that pairing for France.

"I knew it would be difficult after all that success in my first season with Arsenal and then the World Cup. It was unbelievable," says Petit.

"Scoring the final goal in the World Cup was very emotional, too. I had dreamed a long time before that we would win the trophy by beating Brazil in the final 2-0. I did not mind that I got the score wrong!"

He knows that history is against France adding the European crown to that of World champions. It hasn't been done before, although Germany added the World crown to their European title in 1974.

But France know how to deal with pressure and the weight of history. The pressure to deliver World Cup glory two years ago on home soil was immense and Les Bleus can cross the border into neighbouring Belgium and Holland this summer in a more relaxed mood, with that in mind.

On the other hand, Petit warns: "Everyone will be out to beat us simply because we are the reigning World champions."

Petit almost quit the English Premiership after his first month because he did not think he could cope with the physical or mental demands.

But, he says: "I think the last years have taught me a lot about myself. Most importantly, that I like to win. It is a fantastic feeling and the more success you have, the more you want."

Euro2000 verdict: A fit and motivated Petit is crucial if France are to relive the dream.

STATS

Born: 22 September, 1970, Dieppe.

Club: Arsenal.

Fee: £3.5m from AS Monaco.

QUOTE

"Scoring in the World Cup final was so emotional."

DID YOU KNOW?

Manu almost quit Arsenal after a month because of the pressure.

adidas
FIFA WORLD CUP
FRANCE 98
17
17

DAN PETRESCU

MIDFIELDER

Dan Petrescu was something of an unknown when he joined Sheffield Wednesday in 1994. But by the time he scored the last-minute goal that almost undid England's last World Cup challenge in the opening group, his reputation had gone before him.

David Pleat didn't rate him much when he took over at Hillsborough and so, in 1995, off-loaded him to Chelsea. Now, after winning the FA Cup, Coca-Cola Cup, European Cup-winners' Cup and playing in the Champions' League, Petrescu is in no doubt that Pleat did him a big favour.

Now he wants to finish his career at Stamford Bridge. "I don't want to play for any other club," the 33-year-old wing-back says.

Last year, with his contract at the club running down, he played like someone wanting a new one sorted out urgently. He scored the only goal of Chelsea's Champions' League clash against Turkish side Galatasaray – a team including a couple of his international team-mates.

"It was my most important goal for Chelsea in five years at the club," Petrescu said at the time. Afterwards he caught up with Gheorghe Hagi and Gica Popescu, mainstays of the Romanian team for years – who both play for Gala.

They talked about Chelsea's inconsistent League form while producing quality performances in Europe. Petrescu put that down to the Blues being a European team.

"Most of us are foreigners and we know how to cope with European teams better," he said. The Premiership was a learning curve. On the international front, while the trio caught up over pasta at a restaurant in London's West End, they looked forward to the clash with England in the teams' final group game in Charleroi on June 20. The Romanians, of course, defeated Glenn Hoddle's side 2-1 when they met in France two years ago and they expect just as tight a game.

"Although it is a new tournament, with many different players, I think the World Cup match will be in some minds and that could have an effect. Certainly for us, we know we can beat England and they know that," says Petrescu.

He said the feeling in the Romanian camp is that all the teams in the group – Portugal and Germany are the others – are very strong and anything could happen. But they have opened the psycho war by playing up England's chances. Petrescu says: "England are one of the strongest teams in the world and I'm sure they will show their great value."

Petrescu is in an ideal place to do a little scouting for his international bosses. He faces England's finest, week-in, week-out. And he sometimes finds himself looking back with wonder at how far he has come since his teenage days in the Steaua Bucharest team with whom he won so many domestic honours and admiration from abroad.

At 33, he might just be thinking he could be a little too old for his energetic role on the right of midfield to make it to the next World Cup, assuming Romania qualify. But he'll put such thoughts from his mind as he sits back and thinks of England – and maybe another late winning goal.

Euro2000 verdict: England will be wary of Dan the man.

STATS

Born: 22 December, 1976, Bucharest.

Club: Chelsea.

Fee: £2.3m, from Sheffield Wednesday November 1995.

QUOTE

"We know we can beat England - and so do they."

DID YOU KNOW?

He has a young daughter named Chelsea!

adidas
2
2

KAREL POBORSKY

MIDFIELD

Karel Poborsky was one of the hottest items on the menu at Euro96. His electric pace and flowing locks made him an easy target for talent spotters, and Manchester United were at the head of the queue.

Sadly his spell at Old Trafford was not a glittering chapter in his career, though he still has fond memories of his time with United.

But he has no regrets about his move to Benfica – only disappointment that the United fans did not see the best of him.

The Czech Republic winger says: "Supporters in England are the best in the world. And the atmosphere at Wembley is unique in the game. Most of our players thought we had played our first and last game there against Germany in the Euro96 final.

"It was great to go back there a couple of years ago in a friendly match, even if we did lose 2-0. I was grateful to United for giving me the chance to play in England. It was my initiation into big-time club football in Europe.

"I would have loved to stay but I'm happy at Benfica. It helps to be playing week in, week out. Right now I'm playing some of the best football of my career."

Poborsky, whose United brief was to deliver down the flank a similar service to Ryan Giggs and David Beckham, still follows the fortunes of United avidly in both Czech and Portuguese newspapers and correctly predicted their European Cup triumph in 1999. "I always believed they had the depth in the squad to win the European title," he says.

The comparisons with Giggs weighed heavily and it was a partial relief for Poborsky when he escaped to Lisbon. He had cost United £3.6m but featured so rarely that he was in danger of not having his work permit renewed by the Government.

He struggled to get to grips with the language, though his wife spoke good English. His biggest battle was getting into the star-studded United line-up. And even £7,000-a-week wages is no compensation if you're sitting on the bench.

Graeme Souness, the former Liverpool skipper and manager, signed Poborsky for Benfica and says the Czech's only failing has been his inconsistency. "On his day," says Souness, "Poborsky is a world-beater. Like many wingers he is totally unpredictable, but when he's on-song he is electrifying. He was brilliant in his first season in Lisbon. In fact, he was one of the main reasons we qualified for the Champions' League.

"If he finds his best form, he'll be a big danger in the European finals."

Euro2000 verdict: Pob's just the job!

STATS

Born: 30 March, 1972, Prague.

Club: Benfica.

Fee: £3.6m from Manchester United, January 1998.

QUOTE

"On his day, Karel is a world-beater."

GRAEME SOUNESS

DID YOU KNOW?

At United he was getting £47,000 a week to sit on the bench.

PUMA
UMBRO
PUMA

JAMIE REDKNAPP

MIDFIELDER

Jamie Redknapp is England's other star midfielder with a pop star wife. But while David Beckham and Posh Spice lead the celebrity lifestyle, Redknapp and his glam other half, Louise, prefer the quiet life. Instead of the flash London restaurants, Redknapp and Louise often go to her mum's for a roast dinner. "Louise often does the cooking – she's a good cook," says Redknapp.

"We're not rock 'n' roll, though we do our share of partying," he says.

Redknapp has had a number of false dawns in his football career. And he hasn't had the chance to be fussy about his opportunities at international level, the most recent being out of position, plugging a hole on the left of midfield – a position no-one has made his own in recent years.

For someone of his ability, it seems odd that the play-off matches against Scotland produced only the 16th cap of his career. But injury has blighted his chances. Redknapp admits: "I'd have to say my England career has been mixed. I remember the Scotland game at Wembley in Euro96. I came on and things went fantastically well for us. I felt I turned the game around but then I fell over when there was no-one near me, hurt my ankle then broke it a year later and ended up out of the England side for two years."

He was made Liverpool captain last year, which underlined Reds' manager Gerard Houllier's faith in his abilities and maturity. The man he replaced was his England team-mate Paul Ince – though the switch did not affect their friendship unduly.

Indeed, Redknapp – son of Harry, the West Ham manager – is a big Ince fan. "He's a winner," he says. "When he's on the top of his game, any team he plays for is a better team for him being around." And Ince returns the compliment, saying: "If anyone had to take over the armband from me, I'm glad it's Jamie. He deserves a decent run in the England side, and I'm sure he'll be relieved if he gets to the finals without being injured – he's had so much bad luck over the years."

One of Redknapp's faults is that he doesn't score enough goals, despite having a lethal shot. His only England goal to date was a long-range screamer in the friendly last year against Belgium. "I connected with that one really well and it just flew in," he recalls. "It was a wonderful feeling scoring for England and it's one I'd like to experience a few more times, especially in a big competition."

That will depend to a large extent on whether Redknapp's injury hoodoo vanishes. And, if England go all the way in Euro2000, it will be a tough call as to where he and Mrs Redknapp celebrate. A Posh do or a roast at mum's? Perhaps they'll do both.

Euro2000 verdict: His big chance to claim a regular place for England.

STATS

Born: 25 June, 1973, Barton-On-Sea.

Club: Liverpool.

Fee: £350,000 from Bournemouth, January 1991.

QUOTE

"Jamie deserves a decent run in the England side."

HARRY REDKNAPP

DID YOU KNOW?

His only England goal came in a friendly against Belgium.

11
11

PETTER RUDI

MIDFIELDER

The disappointment of missing out on the World Cup is still with Petter Rudi. While Norway went on to beat Brazil 2-1 with that late penalty by Kjetil Rekdal in Marseilles, injured Rudi had no option but to work on his fitness and follow matters in France on television.

"It was so frustrating," he recalls. "You never count on things in football, but I had been hoping at least to make the squad for the World Cup. To get injured and miss the trip was a big disappointment."

His £800,000 move from Molde to Sheffield Wednesday in October 1997 had helped his case for selection. The Premiership was just the sort of challenge and provided the higher profile that the Kristiansund-born midfielder needed.

But he took the disappointment in his stride and had a steady if unspectacular season for the Owls the following year. He has since become popular with Wednesday fans for his runs with the ball and his shooting power, though many would say they don't see enough of the latter.

He has won getting on for 30 caps for Norway and at times looks uncomfortable on the field, on account of his height and gait. But Owls fans love to see his positive attitude. He loves to run at defenders. Wednesday boss Danny Wilson might say Rudi needs to work more on his own defensive skills if he is to be a more complete player.

He is a good passer of the ball, works hard on the left of midfield, and he is becoming less afraid to try his luck with a strike at goal from range. "I'd like to see Petter score more goals," says Wilson. "He certainly has a dig on him and hits the target from all sorts of angles and distances in training."

Rudi played his part in Norway's spectacular qualifying campaign in which they were beaten just once and ran away with their group, ahead of Slovenia – and they beat them home and away.

"I'm looking forward to the finals and keeping my fingers crossed that I will stay free from injury and be involved," he says.

Latterly he has seen more action from the bench than as a starter. But Rudi knows that coach Nils Johan Semb likes to see depth in his squad, giving him formation options depending on the opposition.

Come the opener against Spain in Rotterdam on June 13, Rudi might have to settle for a subs' role. But he won't mind – it's better to watch the game from the bench than from the sofa at home.

"The finals could make up a bit for missing the World Cup," he says. And, at 26, he knows the next World Cup is not far away, either.

"We have a strong squad. We look solid at the back and have some exciting options up front. We should be confident of giving a good performance in the finals. We should not worry about any other sides or take anyone for granted."

Euro2000 verdict: Could be a Rudi awakening...

STATS

Born: 17 September, 1973, Kristiansund, Norway.

Clu: Sheffield Wednesday.

Fee: £800,000 from Molde, October 1997.

QUOTE

"I'd like to see Petter score more goals."

DANNY WILSON

DID YOU KNOW?

Petter had to sit out the World Cup through injury.

UMBRO
7
7
UMBRO

EBBE SAND

STRIKER

Danish World Cup striker Ebbe Sand knows the agony as well as the ecstasy. Life could not have been any sweeter for the Brondby boy when he entered the record books for scoring the fastest ever goal as a substitute in the World Cup, 22 seconds after appearing in the 4-1 win over Nigeria.

Just weeks earlier he had been named Danish player of the year for leading new Aberdeen boss Ebbe Skovdah's side to a league and cup Double. He also scored the Danish Superleague's fastest hat-trick in just 11 minutes in November 1997.

He was about to see his club take part in the Champions' League for the first time. But the day after Brondby beat Slovakian champs Kosice to qualify, Sand's world collaped. Doctors found he had cancer and ordered him to undergo an immediate operation to remove a testicle.

Naturally he feared a worse fate. But, a year on, he made a £4m transfer to German club Schalke – and then found fiancée Trine was expecting their first child.

Sand, now 26, remembers visiting his doctor for what he believed would be a routine examination to check out a groin pain which had been troubling him for a couple of weeks.

"The doctor asked me to go for a scan at the hospital and it was there I got the message I had cancer. It was a hammer blow.

"It's very difficult to understand why it's happening to you, especially when I was at the very top of my career.

"Naturally, it was the most difficult time of my life but I understand now that testicular cancer is quite common among men aged 15-40.

"Of course, there is no such thing as a good cancer, but of all the ones to get it was probably the best because there is a recovery rate of almost 100 per cent.

"I was lucky. I left hospital after 14 days and started training straight away and within a week I was playing football again. I remember the joy of scoring my first goal after the operation, two games after I returned to the team.

"However, mentally it took longer to recover – you think a lot about the illness for a long time afterwards."

Sand has since led calls for men to be screened and to increase their awareness of this potential killer, though now his thoughts are beginning to focus on Euro2000.

Kim Vilfort, a member of Denmark's victorious 1992 championship-winning side, has followed Sand's career with interest at Brondby, where he is now a talent scout.

"Ebbe was patient in waiting for his chance at club and international level – but he seems to be trying to make up for lost time now. He's a real talent," says Vilfort.

And former Liverpool and Denmark midfielder Jan Molby, now in management at Kidderminster, says: "Sand has proved that he can do the business at international level. He is the sort of goalscorer the Danes have been seeking for a while. I think he'll have a big impact in the finals."

Euro2000 verdict: Sand takes some shifting...

STATS

Born: 19 July, 1972, Hadsund, Denmark.

Club: Schalke.

Fee: £4m from Brondby, 1999.

QUOTE

"Getting cancer was a real hammer blow."

DID YOU KNOW?

Ebbe scored the fastest World Cup goal as a sub in 1998.

11

PETER SCHMEICHEL
GOALKEEPER

Peter Schmeichel goes to the European Championships with nothing to prove. He has a winner's medal from 1992, a whole shelf-load from his glittering career at Manchester United, and a massive new challenge in Portugal, with Sporting Lisbon. But the 36-year-old is not the kind of player to go into anything in a half-hearted way. He's a winner and he wants to win all the time. Schmeichel is someone who refuses to look back or rest on his laurels.

His farewell game for United was their epic, last-gasp, treble-winning Champions' League final success against Bayern Munich. He refused to talk about retirement after his eight years at Old Trafford, but his aching body told him he couldn't keep up with the demands of being at the top of the Premiership and a move to the sun, in Lisbon, seemed ideal.

It has not proved to be a totally joyful experience. Schmeichel arrived saying that he could help the slumbering giants of the Portuguese League 'do a United'. But within a couple of months Sporting were out of the UEFA Cup, and coach Giuseppe Materazzi quit after pressure from the fans over poor results.

Some of his team-mates did not take well to the typical Schmeichel ear-bashing, which Gary Pallister and later Jaap Stam became accustomed to getting. But the Great Dane is not one to change his ways.

He has at least changed his views on staying in the game after he does give his giant frame a well-deserved rest. "Some years ago, talking to Alex Ferguson, I said I didn't intend to go into coaching.

"But I've thought better of it and can't ever see myself not being connected with football," he says. Indeed, in January he bought Hvidovre, the ailing Danish First Division club where he began his career as a part-timer in 1984. He sees Sir Alex as his role model and possible advisor, and plans a full-time involvement when he quits playing.

Schmeichel loves Portugal and supported their successful bid to host the European Championships in 2004.

Schmeichel played a big role in Denmark's successful qualification for this summer's event, particularly in the historic 3-2 win in Italy that put them back on track. The Danes were 2-0 down and Schmeichel kept Vieri and Inzaghi at bay before they fought back to win with Jon Dahl Tomasson's 63rd-minute strike. "The last half hour was interesting, though," says Schmeichel with customary understatement.

And he sees no reason why Denmark cannot go on to repeat their shock 1992 victory. "No-one expected much of us because we hadn't even qualified," he says. "When Yugoslavia were expelled and we stepped in at the last minute we didn't have time to work out what to expect."

Schmeichel's saves at key moments in the semi-final against Holland and the final against the Germans marked him down as the best keeper in the world.

"We proved ourselves then, and had a good World Cup. People know a bit more about us now, which makes it tougher. But we have good players and the victory in Italy shows that anything is possible from this team," he says.

Euro2000 verdict: It's sad to think this will be Smikes' international farewell.

STATS

Born: 18 November, 1963.

Club: Sporting Lisbon.

Fee: Free from Manchester United, June 1999.

QUOTE

"Anything is possible with this Danish team."

DID YOU KNOW?

Peter recently bought a Danish First Division club.

hummel
FIFA WORLD CUP
FRANCE 98
DBU
1

PAUL SCHOLES

MIDFIELDER

Paul Scholes is a little diamond. That's Sir Bobby Charlton's view of the ginger goal hero whose contribution to England's qualifying campaign was immense.

Sir Bobby is England's all-time leading goalscorer and he bagged a few against the Scots at Hampden Park in his time. But the Manchester United director reckons that Scholes' double there in the Euro2000 play-off first leg were worth their weight in gold. Just like Scholes himself. "He's such a treasure," says Sir Bobby.

"He's not all that big, but he has a habit of getting into dangerous positions and scoring vital goals. It's like defenders forget he's there.

"Watching him score those two goals at Hampden gave me as much pleasure as any goal I scored against Scotland."

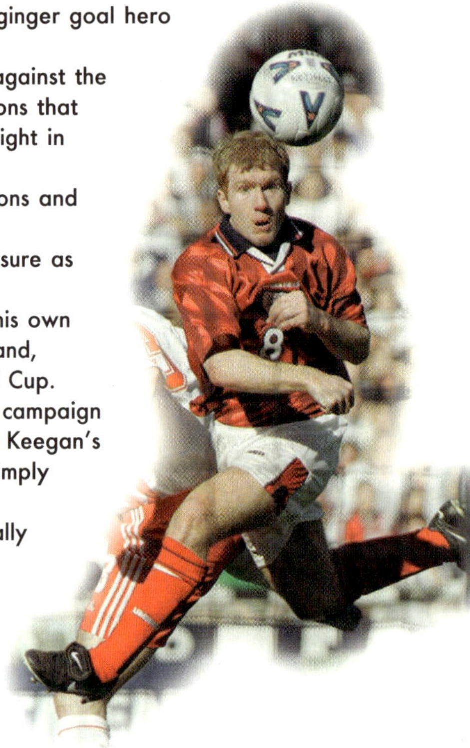

Scholes, a shy, unassuming character, is not one to get carried away by his own publicity. But the plaudits have been stacking up since his first goal for England, against Italy in Le Tournoi de France in 1997, a curtain-raiser for the World Cup.

For the Manchester United terrier, the European Championship qualifying campaign had its fair share of ups and downs. He scored a vital hat-trick to get Kevin Keegan's competitive reign as England coach off to the right sort of start. The Poles simply couldn't deal with his directness and finishing skills that day at Wembley.

But the low-point came when he was sent off against Sweden for a typically robust challenge – he has an impulsive streak that sometimes betrays him when the temperature rises. Being such an important part of Manchester United's treble-winning side has helped him to blossom, though. The only trouble he got into at Hampden came when the Spanish referee booked him for over-celebrating his first goal, putting his hand to his ear to acknowledge the England fans' cheers.

Scholes showed great strength of character in refusing to retaliate after being on the wrong end of a lunging challenge by Scotland's Don Hutchison that Keegan reckoned could have broken his leg.

Keegan admires Scholes – the quiet man of the England camp – and admits he hasn't got to know the little man too well. "Our conversations last about 10 seconds. That's about as much as you get out of him," says the England coach.

Scholes' shyness is such that it cost him a lucrative chance before the World Cup to be in some high-profile TV ads for one of his sponsors, alongside other big stars of the game. He is not one to crave a place on centre stage and he is quick to acknowledge the contributions of others.

"When you get the sort of quality crosses that David Beckham provides, and have players like Michael Owen and Alan Shearer making great runs, there's every chance to get goals. It makes my job easier," says Scholes.

Meanwhile, Scholes is adamant that it is time England started to echo some of Manchester United's achievements. "It is great to win things at club level, but it's about time the national team did it, too. That's something we have every intention of putting right in the finals," he says.

Scholes is approaching peak fitness again after a hernia operation previously scheduled for this summer.

Euro2000 verdict: This ginger one will spice up England's challenge.

STATS

Born: 16 November, 1974, Salford.

Club: Manchester United.

Fee: None. United juniors.

QUOTE

"His goals against Scotland gave me so much pleasure."

SIR BOBBY CHARLTON

DID YOU KNOW?

Paul scored a Wembley hat-trick in the qualifier with Poland.

UMBRO
ENGLAND
11
UMBRO

STEFAN SCHWARZ

MIDFIELDER

Stefan Schwarz became Sunderland's £4m record signing last season as manager Peter Reid headed off a backlash over the departure of talented young striker Michael Bridges to Leeds for £5m. Schwarz, who had a spell at Arsenal earlier in his career, made the switch from Spanish club Valencia to leave Reid excited at his capture and confident that the Swedish midfield star would win over the faithful at the Stadium of Light.

"With his attitude, he's a great asset to any team. If Sweden's game with England at Wembley was anything to go by, our supporters know they have a top-quality player.

The 30-year-old Schwarz effectively replaced Lee Clark, who went to Fulham for £3m. But Reid stressed: "Stefan's not just a playmaker; he puts his foot in as well. You need that in the engine-room.

"He has proved himself in Italy with Fiorentina and in Spain at Valencia. He was outstanding for Benfica against Arsenal, which originally persuaded George Graham to bring him to Highbury."

Schwarz had just one year at Arsenal – 1994-95 – and he says it was not his happiest. But he adds: "I'm older and more mature now. We didn't have the best of seasons at Arsenal. We reached the Cup-winners' Cup Final but were middle of the League." His Portuguese wife, Ceu, didn't settle well in London. That explains why Schwarz has taken so long to decide the Sunderland move was right for him, his wife and two children.

Schwarz's own performances for Sunderland have proved the wisdom of the move and he was instrumental in Sweden's qualifying run, leaving England in their wake.

Against England at Wembley, Schwarz was brilliant, getting his opponents to spill possession and destroying England's probing with his rumbling tackles. Schwarz limped away from Wembley – but he had run the game.

Paul Scholes got no change out of Schwarz – just two bookings and an early bath for fouls on the Swede.

"I don't think I did anything to upset him," Schwarz recalls. "He was a little bit unfortunate about the sending off. But he couldn't complain about getting two yellows for those challenges. It was unlucky for him and unlucky for England. But we were quite pleased."

Sweden will look to the skill and calmness he has shown for Sunderland in recent months. He is remarkably realistic about life, and says: "You have to treat any result the same. If you win, you have to keep your feet on the ground and if you lose, you have to dig a hole in the earth and bury the result."

Schwarz says Sweden are confident of giving a good account of themselves.

"We have a lot of quality in the side but the mentality and character is just as important.

"I don't yearn to be more of a flair player. I'm happy the way I am. I'm competitive and read the game quite well.

"It's always important to be well prepared for games and know a little bit about your opponents," says the man famous in Sweden for maintaining his own training programme – even on holiday. And he'll be prepared for the Euro2000 finals, that's for sure.

Euro2000 verdict: Swede dreams are made of him...

STATS

Born: 18 May, 1969, Kulladahl, Sweden.

Club: Sunderland.

Fee: £4m from Valencia, August 1999.

QUOTE

"I don't yearn to be more of a flair player."

DID YOU KNOW?

He had a disappointing year playing for Arsenal.

adidas
15
adidas

CLARENCE SEEDORF

MIDFIELDER

The Ajax production line that nutured the talents of Clarence Seedorf appears to have dried up. Just as well, Holland's rivals in the European Championship finals might say, after running into him.

The Real Madrid star is one of the most exciting midfielders in the game. He graduated from the famous Ajax soccer school and made his debut for the Dutch giants at just 16. That made him their youngest ever debutant, in 1992.

Fast-striding, beautifully balanced and with a sharp footballing brain, Seedorf has been a major success at Real Madrid, where he collected a Champions' League winner's medal in 1998. That was his second Champions' League success – and with a different club, something few players have achieved. It was in 1995, with Ajax, that he first lifted the most sought-after prize in the club game. By then he had won something like 40 caps for Holland yet was still only a young man in football terms.

Seedorf played for his country in Euro96, though he would prefer to forget England's famous 4-1 hammering of the Dutch in the group clash. He had improved as a player by the time the last World Cup came around and now, with the Euro2000 finals on home soil, he knows he can become a domestic hero once more.

His star faded a little when he left Ajax to join Sampdoria. It was a move doomed to failure. He left Italy after only a year, his confidence dented. But, he says: "I was able to forget that. Clubs such as Real Madrid don't buy poor players. I'd been on the bench at Sampdoria, I didn't get on with the coach, and it was a relief to move to Spain. I've been very happy here ever since."

Those comments fly in the face of reports last summer that he would be joining Lazio after a series of major training ground rows. As it was, Lazio signed the Argentinian, Juan Veron, instead.

Seedorf has had his scrapes with management at the Bernabeu, but then coaches have come and gone at remarkable speed while Seedorf is still standing.

He might have been born on April 1 – but he doesn't suffer fools. He has been involved in controversy with the Dutch squad, too. Together with Patrick Kluivert, Winston Bogarde, Michael Reiziger and Edgar Davids, Seedorf was involved in dressing-room race rows that unsettled the squad in Euro96 and led to Davids being sent home. But, judging by the last World Cup, when the Dutch were semi-finalists, much of the bickering has been put aside. "There is a happier atmosphere in the squad these days," he says of new coach Frank Rijkaard's regime.

Seedorf has never been one to shy away from responsibility. Even missed penalties, which cost him his place in the Dutch side for a time, don't put him off. "I'd take another one if required," he says.

Seedorf is still young enough and important enough to the side to go on to become the Dutch record appearance holder. There will be at least three more to add to the total – their Group D games with the Czech Republic, France and Denmark. And there will be widespread disappointment among the home ranks if the Dutch fail to go any further.

Euro2000 verdict: Classy Clarence is a thriller.

STATS

Born: 1 April, 1976, Paramaribo, Surinam.

Club: Real Madrid.

Previous clubs: Ajax, Sampdoria.

QUOTE

"Clubs like Real Madrid don't buy poor players."

DID YOU KNOW?

Clarence has won the Champions' League with two different clubs.

ALAN SHEARER

STRIKER

Alan Shearer's popularity has taken a huge nosedive since his five-goal heroics in Euro96. In cricket, we are used to England captains being pilloried by fans and written off by the media. But in football it is much rarer – and hardly what coach Kevin Keegan wants as he seeks to get the whole country behind his squad's Euro2000 title bid.

There is no single reason for Shearer's apparent decline, although Keegan still has faith in the Newcastle striker, saying: "He did well enough with Michael Owen in the World Cup. I'm not saying they work fantastic together but I really believe the combination will get better."

Many critics see Shearer as being a yard or two short of his old self – the one that made him a £15m Keegan buy for Newcastle. But that was Shearer before the dreadful knee injury that kept him out of the game for almost a year. The old Shearer scored goals for fun and wasn't left languishing out on the wing.

Yet Shearer was a largely forlorn figure when he led the line for Glenn Hoddle's England. It was Hoddle who took the captaincy from Arsenal's Tony Adams and promoted Shearer.

Jack Charlton, the former England World Cup winner and Republic of Ireland manager, believes Shearer has actually lost relatively little since Euro96. It is more the case that he isn't being used to best effect.

Charlton says: "Shearer is still a quality finisher. He has shown that at Newcastle since Bobby Robson arrived.

"He's just not had the sort of service he needs because England have no natural outlet on the left wing and no-one who can open up defences through the middle, as Paul Gascoigne did.

"I'm convinced that Kevin Keegan knows this and you'll see England get the best out of Shearer at the European finals."

Shearer's critics say he has been a more physical player since his injury – sometimes too much so. Certainly he has had his moments of controversy. But Shearer says he is merely playing the part of the old-fashioned centre-forward and that he should be judged by results – the goals he has been firing in again, especially since Ruud Gullit left the Newcastle manager's chair.

King Al is adamant that the boo boys who have made him a target in recent England games will not upset him in his mission to lead his country to glory in the Low Countries this summer.

"I've come in for some stick from the crowd at Wembley, but I'm not worried. I remember how much they got behind us in Euro96 and I'm sure they can be won over again once the results start coming right.

"I know I'm up to the task and that I'm doing a job to the best of my ability. I have bad days, just like anybody in other walks of life. But I'm focused on seeing England win Euro2000.

"I know we have the players to do it and there is the belief in the squad that we can do it, too. It promises to be an exciting tournament and we're in with as good a chance of winning it as anyone else."

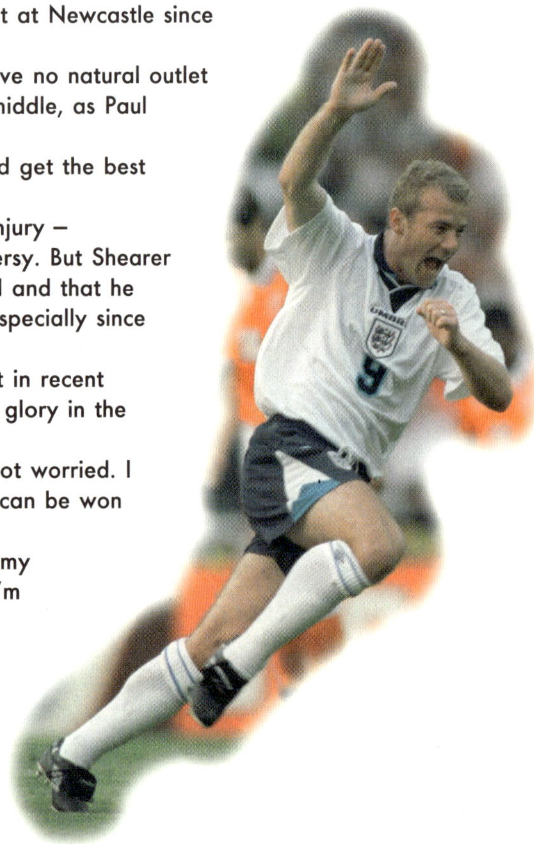

Euro2000 verdict: Shear hell to Shear joy? We'll see...

STATS

Born: 13 August, 1970, Newcastle.

Club: Newcastle United.

Fee: £15m from Blackburn Rovers, July 1996.

QUOTE

"Alan's still a quality finisher."

JACK CHARLTON

DID YOU KNOW?

Shearer is still the most expensive player in English football.

UMBRO
9

VLADIMIR SMICER

STRIKER

Vladimir Smicer has a remarkable wedding tale to tell his grandchildren during his advanced years. He spent his honeymoon at Wembley Stadium, playing the final of Euro96!

He had surprised many by arranging his wedding two days before a certain other big match. The Czechs had surprised still more by beating France on penalties to reach the final.

The Lens striker, who joined Liverpool last year for £4m, married Pavlina Vizek in Prague, where 20,000 fans welcomed the couple at Prague's 13th-century Town Square. The newlyweds then raced back to the Czech team's base in St Albans for Smicer to prepare for the Czech Republic's biggest match in 20 years, against Germany.

Unfortunately, there was no icing on the wedding cake for Smicer. His amazing nuptial dash cost him his starting place against Germany, though he did come on as substitute and almost sealed a stunning victory for the underdogs. Keeper Andreas Kopke scrambled Smicer's 20-yard shot around the post and the Czech dream of emulating the European championship success of their 1976 predecessors ended with Oliver Bierhoff's golden goal.

But it didn't take too much gloss off the occasion for Smicer. "I don't think too many people expected us to reach the final. Just to take part was fantastic. The wedding was memorable, too – to have both in just a few days was incredible!"

He had made his mark in the team when the Czechs looked homeward bound in Euro96 at the group stage, trailing 3-2 to Russia with two minutes left. Smicer levelled the scores with his first international goal. And it hasn't been his last. He has since averaged a goal every other game for his country.

Despite the side's failure to qualify for the last World Cup, Smicer believed the Czechs would bounce back and qualify for Euro2000 in a group containing Scotland.

Arsenal know all about Smicer's skills – he helped send them out of the Champions' League two years ago when he was with Lens. But Liverpool were quick to act when his pal, Reds' midfielder Patrik Berger, said Smicer was keen to team up with him at Anfield. The pair had played together in the Slavia Prague junior team.

Smicer found it hard to settle at Anfield because of a summer injury, but Reds manager Gerard Houlier has kept faith in him, saying. "Vladimir is a good player, everyone can see that. He can take the ball, turn, twist, deliver some good passes, and score.

"Just look at his record with the national team. He was unlucky when he first came here because he had a bad ankle injury and didn't do the pre-season preparation like the others. He was in and out of the squad then because of his injuries. It's tougher in England. It's quicker here, and as he has got used to that he has begun to do the job well.

"No-one should underestimate the Czech team in Euro2000 this summer. They have some very good players and were finalists last time. That sort of experience will help them very much."

Euro2000 verdict: Smicer's a winner – with some help from his Czech mates.

STATS

Born: 24 May, 1973, Prague, Czech Republic.

Club: Liverpool.

Fee: £4m from Lens.

QUOTE

"Injury made it hard for me to settle at Liverpool."

DID YOU KNOW?

He had 20,000 fans at his wedding in 1996!

10
10

OLE GUNNAR SOLSKJAER
STRIKER

Euro2000 gives Ole Gunnar Solskjaer a rare chance to step out of the shadows – and shed his image as Manchester United's supersub.

The 'Baby-faced assassin', as Solskjaer has become known since his £1.5million move from Molde in July 1996, has had to play second fiddle to Dwight Yorke and Andy Cole. But he seldom fails to deliver telling goals when he comes off the bench.

Few have been more important than the last-gasp winner for United against Bayern Munich in the 1999 Champions' League final. United fans have never been surprised by his late interventions. They remember a stunning injury-time goal in the FA Cup against Liverpool that season, which kept their treble dream alive.

The striker grew up in Norway supporting Liverpool and their famed 'Super-Sub' David Fairclough. But Solskjaer says: "I don't want to be remembered as a substitute – I want more games."

Apart from spells when former Norway coach Egil Olsen resorted to long-ball tactics aimed at the giant Tore-Andre Flo, Solskjaer has been a starter for his country. And that's the way he likes it.

He scored crucial goals for the Norwegians in qualifying, notably both efforts in a 2-0 win in Greece, who have been drawn in England's World Cup qualifying group.

He says: "I'm always disappointed to be left out of the team. But I am the kind of player who relies on service, and sometimes the formation we are using requires certain players.

"We are lucky to have so many quality strikers at the moment, like Tore-Andre and Steffen Iversen. It gives the coach a lot of options.

"When you add Harald Brattbakk, Vidar Riseth, Sigurd Rushfelt and now John Carew, who everyone is talking about in Norway, you can see we have a lot of depth when it comes to forward players. That's why I need to be getting regular games for United, just to keep my place in the squad."

Solskjaer believes he has learned so much during his time at Old Trafford and that it is no surprise that the Premiership is a magnet for Scandinavian stars. "We get live English football all the time there. You're brought up on it. And we have the right sort of desire and temperament to do well.

"Having so many talented players at Old Trafford has helped me. I learned so much from Eric Cantona and now Dwight Yorke. A number of the players have been there since they were teenagers, but the majority are my age. That helped me settle in and feel at home.

"There has been talk of moving to other clubs – but United are the best in the world. If you leave, it is hard to see how you can do better for yourself."

As for Norway's chances this summer, Solskjaer says there will be no easy matches. "It is a very open tournament and I can see Slovenia giving us as hard a game as Spain. But we will be confident of doing well and at least getting through the group stage."

Euro2000 verdict: Ole's gunning for glory.

STATS

Born: 26 February, 1973, Kristiansund.

Club: Manchester United.

Fee: £1.5m from Molde, July 1996.

QUOTE

"It's a battle to get a place in the starting line-up."

DID YOU KNOW?

Ole scored on his Norway debut in a 1-1 draw with Jamaica.

UMBRO
UMBRO

PAVEL SRNICEK

GOALKEEPER

Sheffield Wednesday's Czech keeper made his 25th appearance for his country as the Euro96 beaten finalists recorded a crucial victory in Scotland on the way to winning their qualifying group with an unblemished record.

Srnicek lost much of his reputation as an outstanding goalkeeper during the later stages of his spell at Newcastle United. Since moving to Hillsborough, he's had a happier time, even though the Owls have been a largely struggling outfit.

He missed the first five matches of the qualifying campaign and was a non-starter for the Czechs' 2-0 defeat in a friendly at Wembley in November 1998. But, following that tame loss, Srnicek was recalled and saw out the rest of the Euro2000 run as coach Josef Chovanec's first-choice keeper.

That was a source of great delight for Srnicek, who gets the chance to test his skills against some familiar Premiership faces when the Czechs tackle co-hosts Holland, World champions France, and 1992 European champions Denmark in their group matches this summer.

"There are so many of the top stars playing in the Premiership these days," he says. "That includes a growing number of our own team, like Patrik Berger and Vladimir Smicer.

"It's a tough section and at least we will know what to expect from our matches. But we need fear no-one. Qualifying, as we did, with ten wins out of ten will mean nothing in the finals. But it has bred confidence in the squad.

"We know we have world-class players to do it. We are desperate to do even better than Euro96, when I think many people were surprised we reached the final."

Srnicek, who briefly returned to his hometown club Banik Ostrava before joining Wednesday, believes one of the strengths of the Czech side is that they are all true Czechs, even if the majority of the national team pursue careers in foreign leagues – Srnicek included, of course.

"I looked at the Scotland team when we played them in Glasgow and they had a number of English players in the team – players not good enough to play for England.

"I suppose if players don't get the chance to play for their own country then some will take it if another country offers them that chance.

"And it's not just in Scotland that this is happening – it's everywhere. Before the World Cup there were English players who said they were Jamaican and there have been English players in Ireland teams. Even France have included players from their colonies.

"But we are very nationalistic and have strong feelings for the Czech Republic. We are proud of our country. We're real Czechs – and that pride comes through in our matches for our country."

The Czechs conceded just five goals during the qualifying matches and, in Jan Koller, they have someone capable of troubling opposing defences, says Srnicek. "We have a strong squad. We are well organised and I think our group will be very difficult – but the other teams may have more to fear than us."

Euro2000 verdict: Pav and his pals have it all to do.

STATS

Born: 10 March, 1968, Ostrava, Czech Republic.

Club: Sheffield Wednesday.

Fee: Free from Banik Ostrava, November 1998.

QUOTE

"We are real Czechs and our pride shows through."

DID YOU KNOW?

Pavel played for his hometown club, Banik, after leaving Newcastle.

PUMA
PUMA
PUMA

JAAP STAM

DEFENDER

Jaap Stam became the world's most expensive defender when Manchester United paid a stunning £10.75m for the giant stopper from PSV Eindhoven of Holland in May 1998.

United fans got their first look at him during the World Cup, when the Dutch reached the semi-finals. Stam looked caught for pace on several occasions. It brought a raft of criticism, with fans and pundits wondering if this Orange, as the Dutch team are known, was a complete lemon.

A dodgy opening performance for the Reds in a Charity Shield defeat by Arsenal at Wembley did little to help his confidence – but he has since won over his critics. Not that he had many of those in Holland, where Stam was the Dutch Player of the Year and a fixture in the national team. PSV built their side around his defensive talents.

But Stam is taking nothing for granted – even after his treble-winning success with United in 1999, to which Sir Alex Ferguson's team added the intercontinental crown with victory in Tokyo over Palmeiras, the South American champions, last autumn. The FIFA club world championship disappointment in Brazil was a rare blemish on the Red's record.

Stam knows he can expect fierce competition from the rising star of Dutch football – Bert Konterman, who plays for Feyenoord. The pair actually played together at PEC Zwolle, Leewarden and Willem II before Stam's departure to PSV in 1996, so they know each other well.

Konterman made his debut for Holland in a friendly against Argentina, when he did a brilliant job marking the dangerous Gabriel Batistuta. That performance underlined him as Stam's understudy, and the United man says: "I can't take my place for granted at all. Bert is a very talented player and it is probably good for the team that we have this competition for places."

The 6ft 3in stopper was plagued for a time in his first season with United by an achilles tendon injury, but that soon cleared, enabling him to continue to be a central figure in the Reds' defence. It was thought United would have big problems replacing Gary Pallister and Steve Bruce. But Stam has been immovable – a major obstacle for opposing strikers.

As for this summer's big test, Stam knows that the Dutch will be hard pressed to produce victory on home soil. "There will be a lot of pressure on us," he says. "But if we do what we did in the World Cup, concentrate on ourselves, only think about the next game and ignore what others are saying, we should do well."

He can expect a tough time from the Czechs, in particular Vladimir Smicer and Patrik Berger, who play for United's fierce rivals Liverpool. World champions France may pit his old Arsenal opponent Nicolas Anelka against him, while there will be many familiar Premiership faces when Holland play Denmark, who complete their opening group.

"It does help knowing so many players from the Premiership, and we will be well prepared for every game. The expectation will be very high back home though I am sure we can deliver, with the talent we have in the squad," says Stam.

Euro2000 verdict: Stam could be the defensive star of the tournament.

STATS

Born: 17 January, 1972, Kampen.

Club: Manchester United.

Fee: £10.75m from PSV Eindhoven.

QUOTE

‘We can deliver the title on home soil.’

DID YOU KNOW?

United made Jaap the world's most expensive defender.

BRANKO STRUPAR

STRIKER

Belgium's Super Strupar came along at the right time for the Red Devils – but the Euro2000 co-hosts came a bit unstuck in hoping he might be a secret weapon at this summer's finals.

Strupar was largely unknown until Derby County manager Jim Smith made a £3m move for a man who has averaged almost a goal a game for his former club, Racing Club Genk, and his adopted country.

Yes, adopted country. Strupar is not a native Belgian. The giant target man was actually born in Croatia. But he had been playing for Genk – relative newcomers on the major stage – since 1994 and took out Belgian citizenship. That meant that, as a European Union subject, he didn't need a work permit when the Rams butted in to lure him to Pride Park last December in a surprise swoop. By then he'd scored more than 120 goals for Genk and four in five starts for a struggling Belgium national side. They had been in desperate need of a striker after troubled Gilles De Bilde fell out of favour and his former PSV Eindhoven team-mate Luc Nilis retired from international football. That pair are back in harness, but in-form Strupar will take some shifting.

Strupar, who is 6ft 2in and ideally built for a target man, helped Genk qualify for the Champions' League last season for the first time in their brief history following a narrow Belgian League championship win in 1999.

Genk's assistant manager is the long-time international star defender Eric Gerets – a man tipped to coach the national team one day. He said he was sad to see Strupar leave but the money would help Genk build on their unexpected success – the league crown coming just 11 years after the club was founded.

"Three million pounds is a lot of money for a Belgian team, especially for a player of almost 30 years old," said Gerets. "For us it's important to grow as a club so this money will be very useful."

Strupar got his big Premiership chance only when Esteban Fuertes, Derby's Argentinian signing, was discovered to be holding a fake passport and not allowed back in the country after a foreign trip.

Rams boss Jim Smith says he had Strupar in his sights for next season, but the pressure of lack of goals and the Fuertes incident moved him up the priority list. "He can hold the ball well and score goals," said Smith.

Strupar missed a penalty and was sent off for picking up two yellow cards when Smith went to watch him in action for Genk, but the Rams boss stuck to his guns enough to make Strupar, with Craig Burley, his record buy.

"Branko wanted the chance to play in the Premiership and if he's doing well here, I'm sure it'll enhance his chances with the Belgian national team," said Smith.

Euro2000 verdict: Strupar trooper can give Red Devils a cutting edge.

STATS

Born: Croatia.

Club: Derby County.

Fee: £3m from RC Genk (Belgium), December 1999.

QUOTE

'He can hold the ball up well and score goals.'

JIM SMITH

DID YOU KNOW?

Branko was born in Croatia, but is an 'adopted' Belgian.

10

HAKAN SUKUR

STRIKER

Hakan Sukur is a Turkish delight who finds himself right at the front of the shop window at Euro2000. It is a wonder that the little striker is still with Galatasaray.

Sukur-man helped to end the Republic of Ireland's hopes of reaching the Euro2000 finals – and he made short work of AC Milan in last season's Champions' League.

His goals for the men in red and yellow made sure the mightly Italians failed to qualify for the second phase of the Champions' League and were even denied a second European chance in the UEFA Cup.

Sukur is, quite simply, a striking sensation – a 28-year-old goal machine.

He is in his second spell with the Turkish champions following his time with Torino – Juventus's lower-profile Turin rivals. He played only five games for Torino before being shipped back to Turkey amid claims that the Italians could not afford the transfer fee.

It is widely reckoned that Sukur is worth around £12m – and he is sure to be a major transfer target this summer, especially if he has a good tournament. His strength is his bravery in the box. But he also has very quick reflexes, particularly when presented with a half-chance. He is a wily customer, capable of winning penalties against less switched-on opponents, and readily gets under a defender's skin.

Sukur says he wants to stay in Turkey, particularly after his last foreign venture. "I have won a lot of honours in Turkey, but I really want to win a European trophy with Galatasaray – that is my burning ambition.

"My experience with Torino left a very sour taste – but how can people say that I flopped in Italy? I was never given a chance and politics took over.

"But I wasn't unhappy to come home. Galatasaray are my club and I am a far better player than when I left Turkey the first time."

He is happy that his club have shown a decent level of ambition – last season they signed Brazilians Marcio Santos, Capone and Giovanni. "This is the most exciting time I can remember at the club," he says.

In just over 100 league games for his club Sukur has scored around 70 goals, and he averages better than a goal every other game for Turkey.

"With the players we have, Turkey can make a real impact this summer. We certainly want to make up for the disappointment of Euro96, when we didn't perform," he says.

Italian clubs are not the only ones with Sukur's name on their shopping list. Leeds United and Newcastle United are said to be among a number of top Premiership clubs taken with his talents and eye for goal.

And Chelsea's Jes Hogh is a fan. The Dane played for a time in the Turkish League and says: "They call Sukur the Bull of the Bosphorus. It's quite an apt name as he's a real handful."

Euro2000 verdict: Hakan can make a name for himself.

STATS

Born: 1 September, 1971, Adapazari, Turkey.

Club: Galatasaray.

Previous club: Torino, left 1996 for £800,000.

QUOTE

"The Bull of the Bosphorus will be a real handful."

DID YOU KNOW?

He averages better than a goal a game for Turkey.

9
adidas

JON DAHL TOMASSON

STRIKER

Jon Dahl Tomasson has turned his career round in spectacular fashion since his days as a Newcastle United misfit. He had 12 nightmare months at St James' Park after a hugely promising spell in Dutch football – and now the young Danish striker is looking forward to his first major international tournament.

He blames former Newcastle boss Kenny Dalglish for the loss of form that cost him his chance to play for Denmark in the last World Cup. "Dalglish used me as a target man and this is not my position. I played only two matches in my own position, so what did Newcastle expect?

"I had hoped that I would do well playing alongside Alan Shearer, but he was out until the new year with his leg injury and we tried all sorts of different formations. It was unsettling for the team and we struggled badly in the league. I had been looking forward to playing with Shearer, but we started just a handful of games together."

Copenhagen-born Tomasson left Tyneside in a £2m move to Feyenoord, of Rotterdam, and he's looking forward to Euro2000, which is being played partly on his adopted home soil. "I went to Newcastle expecting beautiful things but it all turned out very badly for me and I was very disappointed.

"Because of what happened at Newcastle, I lost my place in the Danish World Cup squad, and that will always be a painful memory of my time there."

Tomasson was the Danes' top scorer during their run to Euro2000, and was on target in both their play-off clashes with Israel, which they breezed 8-0 on aggregate. The first leg, a 5-0 win, left former coach Bo Johansson applauding a perfect performance. The Danes took control in Tel Aviv after only two minutes, Tomasson latched on to Ebbe Sand's pass to score. He added a second before half-time.

Earlier in the campaign, Tomasson scored his first ever international goal as the Danes ended Wales' forlorn hopes of qualifying for the finals, to disappoint joint Welsh bosses Neville Southall and Mark Hughes.

Tomasson had been on the pitch at Liverpool's Anfield ground for only 14 minutes when he scored after a terrible mis-punch by keeper Paul Jones from Chris Coleman's back-header. Tomasson compounded the Welsh misery when he won a debatable late penalty under challenge from Coleman, and Stig Tofting converted.

"We have a very tough group now with Holland, France and the Czechs. I think we will be the underdogs. But no-one gave Denmark a chance in 1992 and we won it. It was a remarkable achievement for football in such a small country and it would be wonderful if we could repeat that achievement this summer," he says.

"It is a very open tournament and it will be down to the team that has the most fit players and finds its form quickest."

Euro2000 verdict: Under-rated star who has regained his best form.

STATS

Born: 29 August, 1976, Copenhagen.

Club: Feyenoord

Fee: £2m from Newcastle United, June 1999.

QUOTE

"Newcastle never gave me a chance to show my skills."

DID YOU KNOW?

He was the Danes' top scorer in reaching the Euro2000 finals.

hummel
9

GIOVANNI VAN BRONCKHORST

MIDFIELDER

Giovanni van Bronckhorst is the man with the Italian-sounding name who plays his club football in Scotland but is a Dutch international. Well, that's the European Union working at its best!

Van Bronckhorst was one of two signings made by Rangers boss Dick Advocaat from the Dutch squad which reached the semi-finals of the World Cup in France. He recently pledged his future to the Glasgow club after Atletico Madrid bid £7m for him.

But, unlike his Rangers team-mate, former PSV midfielder Arthur Numan, van Bronckhorst, formerly of Feyenoord, spent the World Cup finals on the bench. He knows, though, that his time will come. At 25, he is now an established international – one sure to have a big future.

Advocaat had to beat the attention of several clubs to land van Bronckhorst in a £5.25m deal, and the player immediately repaid a large slice on his Rangers debut at left back. He scored in the 5-3 UEFA Cup victory over Shelbourne. But van Bronckhorst is more at home in midfield, and was switched back for the return match. He has been a consistent performer for 'Gers all season, as well as for Holland. The move has done him no harm, since Advocaat, a power in the Dutch game for many years, has been able to press the player's claims with new coach Frank Rijkaard. He has made him a fixture in his international squads, and he featured in the recent friendlies against co-hosts Belgium (a 5-5 draw) and Brazil, which finished 2-2.

Rijkaard would like to have seen the youngster in a more competitive environment, but the Dutch have been confined to friendly fixtures as hosts of Euro2000 and thus not needed to battle through the qualifying groups.

But he saw enough against the Brazilians to know that van Bronckhorst has enormous potential and brings some youth to a side built around the old Ajax academy's graduates. Younger blood will be needed for the World Cup and van Bronckhorst fits the bill.

Advocaat is a huge fan of the player and says: "I believe he will be a big influence and that is why I bought him." He is a commanding player who has a great physical presence about him in midfield and he can also score goals, as he showed in the Champions' League last season.

Van Bronckhorst has drafted in the help of a fitness coach, Ezy McKenzie, in order to press his claims for a place in Euro2000.

It had nothing to do with being fit for his recent marriage to Marieke Wolfers in Rotterdam. Rather, the course, in Florida, was designed to help with balance and poise.

McKenzie, whose professional career was ended by injury at 20, said his mobility exercises could not be more removed from the traditional football training diet of running around cones or through ladders on the ground. Instead, he focuses on exercises that quicken foot movement and improve mobility.

He uses a specialist 'soft' floor that imitates the sensation of running through quicksand. He puts his clients through rigorous running, stretching and balancing routines on different surfaces – from rigid artificial floors to natural grass.

Well that should help when Holland open up against the Czechs in Amsterdam on June 11.

Euro2000 verdict: The future is Orange for Giovanni...

STATS

Born: 5 February, 1975, Rotterdam.

Club: Glasgow Rangers.

Fee: £5.2m from Feyenoord, July 1999.

QUOTE

"He will be a big influence."

DICK ADVOCAAT

DID YOU KNOW?

'Ballet' exercises have helped his poise and fitness.

EDWIN VAN DER SAR
GOALKEEPER

Edwin Van Der Sar was the man widely touted to replace Manchester United legend Peter Schmeichel when the great Dane left Old Trafford a year ago. Instead, the brilliant Dutchman – arguably the best keeper at the last World Cup – opted for Juventus.

In one sense it was an obvious move. Juve are one of the world's biggest clubs – if not as wealthy or popular as United. The down side was that the 1998 winners had failed to qualify for the Champions' League – a competition in which they have been fixtures over the years.

Van Der Sar was looking long term. He's 30, and that is arguably still short of full maturity for a top-class goalkeeper.

United were never going to break their wages structure for a keeper. It took all of Roy Keane's muscle, amid overtures from Juventus, to crack it. And Van Der Sar wanted to test himself in the best league in the world – Serie A.

So, having won the Champions' Cup with Ajax, and very much more in his time at the Amsterdam club, Van Der Sar chose the culture and climate of the Stadio delle Alpi ahead of rainy afternoons playing snooker in Manchester.

Van Der Sar still had European football on the agenda – a beefed-up UEFA Cup – and the opportunity to play alongside the likes of Zinedine Zidane, Alex Del Piero and his Dutch team-mate Edgar Davids.

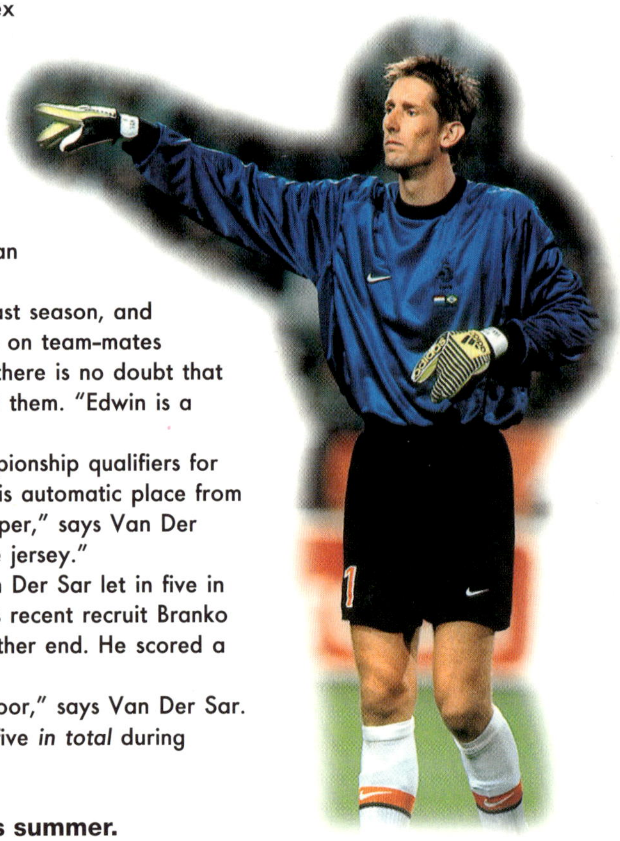

Indeed, once the offer came, Van Der Sar got the lowdown on Juve from Davids.

"The club sold itself, but Edgar was able to give me some information on life in Turin and the problems I might face," said Van Der Sar.

He has warmed to his task, and is enjoying facing the likes of Andrei Schevchenko (Milan), Gabriel Batistuta (Fiorentina), Christian Vieri and Ronaldo (Inter) on a regular basis.

Juve fielded one of the meanest defences in the Italian League last season, and Van Der Sar was one of the reasons. He is quick to shower praise on team-mates Ciro Ferrara, Gianluca Pessotto and young Croat Igor Tudor, but there is no doubt that they in turn have enjoyed the security of the big Dutchman behind them. "Edwin is a very safe pair of hands," says Pessotto.

Van Der Sar played in the vast majority of the European Championship qualifiers for Holland, though he finds himself getting growing competition for his automatic place from Sander Westerwald, of Liverpool. "Sander is a very good goalkeeper," says Van Der Sar. "It is good for the team that we have this competition for the jersey."

Even the best of keepers can have his odd off-day, though. Van Der Sar let in five in a friendly late last year against Belgium, two coming from Derby's recent recruit Branko Strupar. It rather undid the good work of Patrick Kluivert at the other end. He scored a hat-trick in a bizarre 5-5 draw.

"You could not blame any one person that day. We were all poor," says Van Der Sar. Any spare pocket money should be wagered that he won't let in five *in total* during Euro2000.

Euro2000 verdict: Big Ed's the best keeper on show this summer.

STATS

Born: 29 October, 1970, Holland.

Club: Juventus.

Fee: £6.5m from Ajax, June 1999.

QUOTE

"Edwin is a very safe pair of hands."

GIANLUCA PESSOTTO

DID YOU KNOW?

Edwin once scored a goal for his former club Ajax.

PATRICK VIEIRA

MIDFIELDER

Few players in the Premiership have had as controversial a career as Patrick Vieira. Red and yellow cards have littered his path. But Arsene Wenger, his manager at Arsenal, would say that this is a testament to Vieira's rugged determination and effectiveness as a combative midfielder.

He must be the most imposing figure to line up against. This young Frenchman is the perfect athlete, giant of frame and superbly muscled. At 24 – his 25th birthday falls during the quarter-finals of Euro2000 – Vieira is already a World Cup winner. One of a very select band, indeed.

It was his trademark pass to team-mate Emmanuel Petit that crowned France's glory in Paris, setting up the third goal and igniting the celebrations as the hosts beat the most famous of football nations, Brazil, for their first ever world title.

As if that in itself was not enough, Vieira had already become a Premiership and FA Cup Double winner with Arsenal that spring. If things have levelled out for the leggy youngster since then, perhaps that is not too surprising.

He says it has been hard to come to terms with so much success so early in his career. Not that he feels under-motivated. More that it has been difficult to find his peak form since then. Too little rest after the World Cup, combined with injuries and suspensions. It has been stop-start for Vieira and another summer of pressure, and lack of rest might have him in two minds right now.

He says he's looking forward to the challenge of Euro2000 – particularly June 21 in Amsterdam, when France's clash with Holland promises to be one of the most attractive ties imaginable. It pits Vieira and Petit against their Gunners pals Marc Overmars and Dennis Bergkamp.

"Yes, that should be quite an evening," he says with a certain understatement. "We are always friends but for a time we will not be. Afterwards we will be friends again. Hopefully we will both get the result we need to go on in the competition. But it is a very difficult group. The Czech Republic and Denmark will not be easy."

Vieira was the first piece in Wenger's Arsenal jigsaw, arriving at Highbury in a £3m switch from AC Milan even before the manager himself. The Senegal-born midfielder arrived as an unknown but he left his mark very quickly – on opposing players, and also in the hearts of the Highbury crowd who adore him.

Vieira loves big occasions. He was disappointed to miss the 1996 Olympics with torn knee ligaments that kept him out for the game for three months, but the World Cup was "a dream come true".

Now he has a chance to add a European championship winner's medal to his growing collection and there is confidence that he can do better than Arsenal have in European competition themselves in recent seasons.

"France, of course, play differently. But everyone at Arsenal is surprised and disappointed not to have done better in Europe. I am sure that if England cannot win the tournament, we will have much support from Arsenal fans as we French try to win the trophy."

Short-fused. Doesn't get enough goals. We've all heard the criticisms. Yet Patrick Vieira could be quite some player when he is the finished article.

Euro2000 verdict: Must keep his temper in check.

STATS

Born: 23 June, 1976, Dakar, Senegal.

Club: Arsenal.

Fee: £3m from AC Milan, July 1996.

QUOTE

"Playing against Bergkamp and Overmars will be some night!"

DID YOU KNOW?

Patrick was captain of Cannes when he was only 19.

CHRISTIAN VIERI

STRIKER

When the Italian side stands to sing the national anthem before an international, listen closely as the camera homes in on Christian Vieri. You can't miss him. He's the only one singing with an Australian accent!

Actually, it's not so pronounced nowadays. After all, he was 14 when he left his home Down Under to live with his grandmother in Italy. And he recalls that he was so unhappy that he cried all the time, and called his dad, begging to go back to Australia. Luckily for club and country, when Vieri did finally go back he felt homesick again – this time for Italy. So back to Italia he went.

Vieri has since gone on to become one of the hottest names in Italy and was the toast of France98, when he came close to finishing top marksman, only to be outdone by Davor Suker of Croatia.

He has played for eight clubs in just eight years, becoming the most expensive player in the history of the game when he left Atletico Madrid last year for Inter Milan, who paid a staggering £31m for him. That put even his new team-mate Ronaldo in the shade. Clubs have been queuing for his signature and falling over themselves to shell out massive money for his talents. Lazio paid £18m. Atletico spent £12m.

The one constant in his career is that almost every year Juventus try to get him back. He arrived at Juve aged 23 and far from the finished article. But he worked hard. "They sorted me out technically and tactically," Vieri recalls.

They thought they had their man but instead he joined Lazio. It was too good a deal, even though he regrets not getting to play alongside his great pal and international strike partner Filippo Inzaghi and the inimitable Zinedine Zidane.

He's happy at Inter, where he describes teaming up with Ronaldo as 'the stuff of dreams – a fantasy scenario', even if the great Brazilian has been a shadow of his former self because of injury.

"I can learn so much from Ronaldo," he says. "I joined Inter to improve as a player."

Vieri and Inzaghi are national team coach Dino Zoff's first-choice pairing up front, though a fit-again Alex Del Piero is a threat to both of them. But Vieri says "Pippo and I are inseparable. Every time we play together, we score. We work well together and I think things should be left as they are."

Vieri, nicknamed Bobo, believes Italy have more than enough class to lift the European title. "We have the best team in the world right now. We have the best goalkeeper – Buffon; the best defenders – Maldini, Nesta, Panucci and Cannavaro; the best attackers – Del Piero, Inzaghi and Totti – and the best midfielders, too.

"We did well enough in qualifying for the finals, but then you don't get prizes for winning every qualifying game. If you check the records, you'll see that Italian teams save their best for the final rounds."

Euro2000 verdict: Vieri hot prospect to be top goalscorer.

STATS

Born: 12 July, 1973, Bologna.

Club: Inter Milan.

Fee: £31m from Atletico Madrid.

QUOTE

"Italy are the best team in the world right now."

DID YOU KNOW?

Christian lived in Australia until he was 14 - and was good at cricket.

21
FIFA WORLD CUP
FRANCE
21

MARC WILMOTS

MIDFIELDER

Belgian veteran Marc Wilmots can't wait for the big summer show. But he is praying that hooligans don't ruin the tournament that his country has worked long and hard to co-host.

Unrest among fans in Germany last season prompted Wilmots to sound a warning note. He plays his club football with Schalke in Germany and he remembers only too vividly how German fans brought shame to the last World Cup, when a French policeman was almost killed by rioting in Lens.

Wilmots, who played in the World Cup and impressed last year for the Belgians at Wembley, says: "Belgium and Holland are only small countries. If hooligans come in from England, Italy and Germany then it will be dangerous. The organisers are doing what they can.

"They are registering the name and address of the purchaser of every ticket. Cars won't be allowed anywhere near the stadia and buses will be laid on to try to keep the fans under tighter control. But what really scares me is the thought of what may happen in the streets after the matches."

Wilmots pinpoints the De Kuip in Rotterdam which is, worryingly, the venue for the Euro2000 Final, as a prime potential trouble spot.

Last season saw matches postponed in Belgium because of hooligan threats, rioting in Rotterdam and renewed problems at German matches.

But Wilmots, for all his fears, believes it will pass off peacefully and looks forward to a feast of football – with Belgium unfancied but improving fast at just the right time.

Wilmots won the UEFA Cup with Schalke in 1997, so he's had some European success.

"We might only be 32nd in the world rankings but we have some very good players coming through. Branko Strupar has done well since his move to England and we look like we might have some forwards who could cause other teams some problems," says Wilmots.

"I have read much about us not being good enough to reach the finals had we not been hosts. But I believe we have been through a transition since the World Cup and things are at last beginning to take shape for the coach."

Wilmots has been central to new coach Robert Waseige's tactical thinking and certainly his experience at international level will be crucial for a young Red Devils side.

He hopes for a Holland v Belgium final. Not least because the last clash, a 'friendly' last year, ended in a bizarre 5-5 draw in Rotterdam which saw 10 players booked and Wilmots sent off.

Wilmots scored one of his side's goals, while Patrick Kluivert bagged a hat-trick and still wasn't on the winning side! "I think that would make a very interesting rematch," he says, mischievously.

Euro2000 verdict: He'll keep Belgium up to the Marc.

STATS

Born: 22 February, 1969, Dongelberg, Belgium.

Club: Schalke 04.

Previous clubs: Mechelen, St. Truiden, Standard Liege.

QUOTE

"My dream is for Belgium to play Holland in the Euro2000 final."

DID YOU KNOW?

He was sent off for the first time in a 5-5 draw with Holland last year.

ZLATKO ZAHOVIC

MIDFIELDER

You might not have heard of too many Slovene footballers. But then neither have many Slovenes themselves! Until recently, ski jumping and basketball have dominated the sports pages in this tiny mountainous country – population around two million.

Zlatko Zahovic is the David Beckham of this country which became independent from Yugoslavia in 1991 and is generally well behind its neighbours, Croatia, Bosnia and Macedonia in football's pecking order.

Until now, even Zahovic, whose efforts have almost single-handedly taken the Slovenes to their first major football event, has ranked well behind twice-overall World Cup ski jumping champion Primoz Peterka.

Zahovic has played for several major clubs in Europe. First he was with Partizan Belgrade, in Yugoslavia. They were a dominant force in the early 1990s, winning the Yugoslavian Cup and two league Championships.

The talented attacking midfielder then tried his luck abroad, in Portugal, playing first for relative unknowns Guimaeres before, 12 months later, being snapped up by Porto when former England manager Bobby Robson was in charge.

He formed a lethal partnership with the Brazilian striker, Jardel, Portugal's golden boot on several occasions. Manchester United fans may recall facing this pair in the Champions' League, though Eric Cantona and Ryan Giggs blew them away on a memorable night at Old Trafford.

Nevertheless, Zahovic bagged seven goals for the Portuguese top dogs in the 1998-99 Champions' League campaign. In all he collected three Portuguese titles before a lucrative move last year to Olympiakos, of Greece.

The Greeks had been alerted to his abilities when Zahovic scored twice in a come-from-behind draw in a Euro2000 qualifier in Athens in October 1998. They were crucial goals, because coach Srecko Katanec's team battled back brilliantly to pip the Greeks for the play-off place behind section winners Norway.

Zahovic is his country's leading scorer with 20 goals from 41 matches. And he warns that Slovenia aren't going to the finals – in which they have been drawn again with Norway – just to make up the numbers.

He says: "I hear that the odds are 80-1 against us. Bet on Slovenia and you will earn a lot of money.

"Our coach says we deserved to qualify because we worked hard for it, we played well and we dared to be courageous throughout the qualification. He was right."

Slovenia lost twice to Norway and once to Greece during qualifying but made the finals with an unexpected 3-2 aggregate victory over Ukraine in the play-offs.

Zahovic says there is a superb spirit in the camp. "The coach is always clear in his message that we will only be able to achieve good results if we are all good friends and play with our hearts. That is how we intend to surprise everyone this summer."

Euro2000 verdict: Watch out for the quick, quick Slovene!

STATS

Born: 1 February 1971, Maribor.

Club: Olympiakos.

Previous clubs: Hadjuk Split, Vittoria, Porto.

QUOTE

"We intend to play with our hearts and surprise you all."

DID YOU KNOW?

Slovenia came into existence only in 1991.

10
10

ZINEDINE ZIDANE
MIDFIELDER

Two goals in a World Cup Final – that doesn't look too bad on the old career record, does it? But some critics believe that Zinedine Zidane, given his wonderful array of skills, his vision and his touch, should have won far more.

A World Cup – yes, even the biggest prize in the game is scant reward, they say, for his talents. Two losing Champions' League finals with Juventus, a losing UEFA Cup Final with Bordeaux and a dreadfully disappointing Euro96 with France. They have all been thrown in Zidane's face by those who accuse him of faltering when the really serious questions are being posed.

El Zid is quick to counter that he is 'not a jinx', though the serious judges reckon Zidane is only as good as he is allowed to be and that he needs a quality 'minder' – someone to fetch and carry for him and protect him from the rough stuff – to be at his best.

Didier Deschamps did just that in France98 when the hosts reigned supreme, beating Ronaldo and Co. in the final. The ruthlessly effective dreadlocked Dutchman, Edgar Davids, does it for Juventus.

"Put Deschamps and Zidane in a blender and you'd have the perfect mix," is FA technical boss Howard Wilkinson's view.

Manchester United boss, Sir Alex Ferguson, had Zidane as his prime candidate to replace Eric Cantona and in 1995-96 had him watched almost a dozen times. But he could not tempt him to Old Trafford. "I could never decide his best position," was Sir Alex's opinion. "I had him marked down as a front player, but at Juventus and for his country he has developed brilliantly as a midfielder."

Zidane can't wait for the big stage this summer to nail some of his critics. He feels the European Championships should see him at his best. In 1996 he went into the tournament a spent force after a year of uninterrupted football that began the previous summer in the InterToto Cup and ended in a UEFA Cup final defeat just before he headed to England.

Then, a fortnight before Euro96 began, Zidane was in a car crash. "My form was poor," he recalls. "I could not lift myself and was suffering from intense fatigue."

Zidane fought back to become a World Cup hero two years later, despite being sent off against Saudi Arabia, missing two matches, including the golden goal win over Paraguay. He felt as tall as the giant poster of him on the side of a house in his native Marseilles. That and a second Italian League title and the World Player of the Year award should have been all the ammunition he needed.

But he's gutsy, Zidane. It comes from his teenage dilemma – should he give up judo or football in order to save the wear and tear on his growing body?

Forget the critics, Zinedine... the rest of us know you made the right choice.

Euro2000 verdict: France will go close with the Z-man at his best.

STATS

Born: 23 June, 1972, Marseilles.

Club: Juventus.

Fee: £3.2m from Bordeaux, July 1996.

QUOTE

"Put Zidane and Deschamps in a blender to make the perfect player."

HOWARD WILKINSON

DID YOU KNOW?

Manchester United wanted Zidane to replace Eric Cantona.

adidas
10
10

CHRISTIAN ZIEGE

MIDFIELDER

Christian Ziege reignited his international career with a £4m move from AC Milan to Middlesbrough – and a hat-trick to destroy Northern Ireland as holders Germany qualified for Euro2000.

He became one of the major overseas successes in the Premiership following his transfer to the Riverside Stadium – and his skills at dead-ball situations have impressed even team-mate Paul Gascoigne.

Ziege's career had been on the skids in Milan after losing his place in the Serie A team through injury. The chance to join Bryan Robson's foreign legion on Teesside gave Ziege a big boost. Not only was he able to get regular first-team football again but it helped restore his place in the German national team.

"In Milan it was difficult for me, and I was aware that I would not play for the national team while I could not get regular football there. The move to Middlesbrough came at the right time," he said.

His treble against Northern Ireland was all the justification he needed, and afterwards, the talented wing-back knelt on the turf in prayer. Later he championed the cause of Gazza, saying England coach Kevin Keegan should not overlook him for Euro2000. "I'm not sure I would be so happy with him playing against us, but he is a real talent and England need his sort of skills right now.

"He has done more than enough in the games we have played together, and on the training pitch, to convince me that he is still a class act who can perform on the biggest stage.

"You don't lose ability like his, and I have also been impressed with his enthusiasm. If you are looking for players with that spark of creativity, there are few better, and it is good to see him back in such good form after his injury problems.

"I have had lots of conversations with Paul about football in general and settling into a new lifestyle in a different country, and he has been a great help. I have nothing but admiration for him, and there is no doubt in my mind that he still has plenty to offer."

Ziege recalls how he feared for his own international future and feared his 12-month spell in the international wilderness would continue. ''When Bryan Robson first came in for me, I told him I wanted to stay in Milan and try to make a go of it. But I had to accept I had no future at the San Siro when they made it clear I was not going to get into the team.

"That was when I remembered Bryan's words to me. He had told me I was among the three best left-sided midfield players in the world and that, if I signed for Middlesbrough, he would make sure I got back into the Germany team.

"I owe him so much because there is no way the German manager would have considered recalling me against Finland if I had not been playing for my club side. Now I could not be happier."

Now the 28-year-old has the inside track on England's best players before the crunch tie between the old enemies in Euro2000. "It will be quite some contest and it is difficult to choose between the teams," he says.

Euro2000 verdict: Christian will soldier onwards.

STATS

Born: 1 Febuary, 1972, Berlin.

Club: Middlesbrough.

Fee: £4m from AC Milan, July 1999.

QUOTE

‘Paul Gascoigne's a real talent... you don't lose ability like his.’

DID YOU KNOW?

The move to Middlesbrough rescued Ziege's international career.

17

HOW THEY GOT THERE

The nine group winners qualified automatically. The team with the best runners-up record – Portugal – also qualified by right. The other eight runners-up were drawn in play-offs home and away with the winners on aggregate qualifying for the finals on June 10 to July 2.

*Qualified for play-offs
** Qualified as best runners-up

GROUP 1

Wales 0 Italy 2
Belarus 0 Denmark 0
Italy 2 Switzerland 0
Denmark 1 Wales 2
Wales 3 Belarus 2
Switzerland 1 Denmark 1
Belarus 0 Switzerland 1
Denmark 1 Italy 2
Switzerland 2 Wales 0
Italy 1 Belarus 1
Italy 4 Wales 0
Denmark 1 Belarus 0
Switzerland 0 Italy 0
Wales 0 Denmark 2
Belarus 1 Wales 2
Denmark 2 Switzerland 1
Switzerland 2 Belarus 0
Italy 2 Denmark 3
Wales 0 Switzerland 2
Belarus 0 Italy 0

	P	W	D	L	F	A	Pts
ITALY	8	4	3	1	13	5	15
Denmark *	8	4	2	2	11	8	14
Switzerland	8	4	2	2	9	5	14
Wales	8	3	0	5	7	16	9
Belarus	8	0	3	5	4	10	3

GROUP 2

Georgia 1 Albania 0
Greece 2 Slovenia 2
Norway 1 Latvia 3
Slovenia 1 Norway 2
Latvia 1 Georgia 0
Norway 2 Albania 2
Greece 3 Georgia 0
Slovenia 1 Latvia 0
Albania 0 Greece 0
Greece 0 Norway 2
Georgia 1 Slovenia 1
Latvia 0 Greece 0
Latvia 0 Albania 0
Georgia 1 Norway 4
Norway 1 Georgia 0
Albania 1 Norway 2
Georgia 1 Greece 2
Latvia 1 Slovenia 2
Albania 0 Slovenia 1
Greece 1 Latvia 2
Slovenia 2 Albania 0
Norway 1 Greece 0
Albania 3 Latvia 3
Slovenia 2 Georgia 1
Norway 4 Slovenia 0
Georgia 2 Latvia 2
Greece 2 Albania 0
Albania 2 Georgia 1
Slovenia 0 Greece 3
Latvia 1 Norway 2

	P	W	D	L	F	A	Pts
NORWAY	10	8	1	1	21	9	25
Slovenia *	10	5	2	3	12	14	17
Greece	10	4	3	3	13	8	15
Latvia	10	3	4	3	13	12	13
Albania	10	1	4	5	8	14	7
Georgia	10	1	2	7	8	18	5

GROUP 3

Finland 3 Moldova 2
Turkey 3 N Ireland 0
Turkey 1 Germany 0
N Ireland 1 Finland 0
Moldova 1 Germany 3
Turkey 1 Finland 3
N Ireland 2 Moldova 2
N Ireland 0 Germany 3
Turkey 2 Moldova 0
Germany 2 Finland 0
Moldova 0 N Ireland 0
Germany 6 Moldova 1
Finland 2 Turkey 4
Moldova 0 Finland 0
Finland 1 Germany 2
N Ireland 0 Turkey 3
Germany 4 N Ireland 0
Moldova 1 Turkey 1
Germany 0 Turkey 0
Finland 4 N Ireland 1

	P	W	D	L	F	A	Pts
GERMANY	8	6	1	1	20	4	19
Turkey *	8	5	2	1	15	6	17
France	8	3	1	4	13	13	10
N Ireland	8	1	2	5	4	19	5
Moldova	8	0	4	4	7	17	4

GROUP 4

Armenia 3 Andorra 1
Ukraine 3 Russia 2
Iceland 1 France 1
Andorra 0 Ukraine 2
Russia 2 France 3
Armenia 0 Iceland 0
Ukraine 2 Armenia 0
France 2 Andorra 0
Iceland 1 Russia 0
Andorra 0 Iceland 2
France 0 Ukraine 0
Armenia 0 Russia 3
Ukraine 1 Iceland 1
Russia 6 Andorra 1
France 2 Armenia 0
Ukraine 4 Andorra 0
France 2 Russia 3
Iceland 2 Armenia 0
Andorra 0 France 1
Russia 1 Iceland 0
Armenia 0 Ukraine 0
Ukraine 0 France 0
Iceland 3 Andorra 0
Russia 2 Armenia 0
Andorra 1 Russia 2
Iceland 0 Ukraine 1
Armenia 2 France 3
France 3 Iceland 2
Russia 1 Ukraine 1
Andorra 0 Armenia 3

	P	W	D	L	F	A	Pts
FRANCE	10	6	3	1	17	10	21
Ukraine *	10	5	5	0	14	4	20
Russia	10	6	1	3	22	12	19
Iceland	10	4	3	3	12	7	15
Armenia	10	2	2	6	8	15	8
Andorra	10	0	0	10	3	28	0

GROUP 5

Sweden 2 England 1
Bulgaria 0 Poland 3
Poland 3 Luxembourg 0
England 0 Bulgaria 0
Bulgaria 0 Sweden 1
Luxembourg 0 England 3
Sweden 2 Luxembourg 0
England 3 Poland 1
Luxembourg 0 Bulgaria 2
Poland 0 Sweden 1
Poland 2 Bulgaria 0
England 0 Sweden 0
Luxembourg 2 Poland 3
Bulgaria 1 England 1
Sweden 1 Bulgaria 0
England 6 Luxembourg 0
Luxembourg 0 Sweden 1
Poland 0 England 0
Sweden 2 Poland 0
Bulgaria 3 Luxembourg 0

	P	W	D	L	F	A	Pts
SWEDEN	8	7	1	0	10	1	22
England *	8	3	4	1	14	4	13
Poland	8	4	1	3	12	8	13
Bulgaria	8	2	2	4	6	8	8
Luxembourg	8	0	0	8	2	23	0

GROUP 6

Austria 1 Israel 1
Cyprus 3 Spain 2
Cyprus 0 Austria 3
San Marino 0 Israel 5
San Marino 1 Austria 4
Israel 1 Spain 2
San Marino 0 Cyprus 1
Cyprus 4 San Marino 0
Spain 9 Austria 0
Israel 3 Cyprus 0
San Marino 0 Spain 6
Austria 7 San Marino 0
Spain 9 San Marino 0
Israel 5 Austria 0
Austria 1 Spain 3
Cyprus 3 Israel 2
Israel 8 San Marino 0
Spain 8 Cyprus 0
Spain 3 Israel 0
Austria 3 Cyprus 1

	P	W	D	L	F	A	Pts
SPAIN	8	7	0	1	42	5	21
Israel *	8	4	1	3	25	9	13
Austria	8	4	1	3	19	20	13
Cyprus	8	4	0	4	12	21	12
San Marino	8	0	0	8	1	44	0

GROUP 7

Romania 7 Liechtenstein 0
Slovakia 3 Azerbaijan 0
Hungary 1 Portugal 3
Portugal 0 Romania 1
Liechtenstein 0 Slovakia 4
Azerbaijan 0 Hungary 4
Hungary 1 Romania 1
Slovakia 0 Portugal 3
Liechtenstein 2 Azerbaijan 1
Portugal 7 Azerbaijan 0
Romania 0 Slovakia 0
Hungary 5 Liechtenstein 0
Slovakia 0 Hungary 0
Liechtenstein 0 Portugal 5
Azerbaijan 0 Romania 1
Portugal 1 Slovakia 0
Romania 2 Hungary 0
Azerbaijan 4 Liechtenstein 0
Hungary 0 Slovakia 1
Portugal 8 Liechtenstein 0
Romania 4 Azerbaijan 0
Azerbaijan 1 Portugal 1
Slovakia 1 Romania 5
Liechtenstein 0 Hungary 0
Romania 1 Portugal 1
Slovakia 2 Liechtenstein 0
Hungary 3 Azerbaijan 0
Liechtenstein 0 Romania 3
Azerbaijan 0 Slovakia 1
Portugal 3 Hungary 0

	P	W	D	L	F	A	Pts
ROMANIA	10	7	3	0	25	3	24
Portugal **	10	7	2	1	32	4	23
Slovakia	10	5	2	3	12	9	17
Hungary	10	3	3	4	14	10	12
Azerbaijan	10	1	1	8	6	26	4
Liechtenstein	10	1	1	8	2	39	4

GROUP 8

Rep Ireland 2 Croatia 0
Macedonia 4 Malta 0
Malta 1 Croatia 4
Rep Ireland 5 Malta 0
Croatia 3 Macedonia 2
Malta 1 Macedonia 2
Yugoslavia 1 Rep Ireland 0
Malta 0 Yugoslavia 3
Macedonia 1 Croatia 1
Yugoslavia 4 Malta 1
Rep Ireland 1 Macedonia 0
Yugoslavia 0 Croatia 0
Croatia 2 Malta 1
Rep Ireland 2 Yugoslavia 1
Croatia 1 Rep Ireland 0
Yugoslavia 3 Macedonia 1
Malta 2 Rep Ireland 3
Macedonia 2 Yugoslavia 4
Macedonia 1 Rep Ireland 1
Croatia 2 Yugoslavia 2

	P	W	D	L	F	A	Pts
YUGOSLAVIA	8	5	2	1	18	8	17
Rep Ireland *	8	5	1	2	14	6	16
Croatia	8	4	3	1	13	9	15
Macedonia	8	2	2	4	13	14	8
Malta	8	0	0	8	6	27	0

GROUP 9

Estonia 5 Faroe Is 0
Bosnia-Herz 1 Faroe Is 0
Bosnia-Herz 1 Estonia 1
Lithuania 0 Scotland 0
Faroe Is 0 Czech Rep 1
Bosnia-Herz 1 Czech Rep 3
Lithuania 0 Faroe Is 0
Scotland 3 Estonia 2
Lithuania 4 Bosnia-Herz 2
Scotland 2 Faroe Is 1
Czech Rep 4 Estonia 1
Czech Rep 2 Lithuania 0
Lithuania 1 Estonia 2
Scotland 1 Czech Rep 2
Bosnia-Herz 2 Lithuania 0
Estonia 0 Czech Rep 2
Faroe Is 1 Scotland 1
Estonia 1 Lithuania 2
Faroe Is 2 Bosnia-Herz 2
Czech Rep 3 Scotland 2
Bosnia-Herz 1 Scotland 2
Faroe Is 0 Estonia 2
Lithuania 0 Czech Rep 4
Czech Rep 3 Bosnia-Herz 0
Faroe Is 0 Lithuania 1
Estonia 0 Scotland 0
Scotland 1 Bosnia-Herz 0
Estonia 1 Bosnia-Herz 4
Czech Rep 2 Faroe Is 0
Scotland 3 Lithuania 0

	P	W	D	L	F	A	Pts
CZECH REP	10	10	0	0	26	5	30
Scotland *	10	5	3	2	15	10	18
Bosnia-Herz.	10	3	2	5	14	17	11
Lithuania	10	3	2	5	8	16	11
Estonia	10	3	2	5	15	17	11
Faroe Islands	10	0	3	7	4	17	3

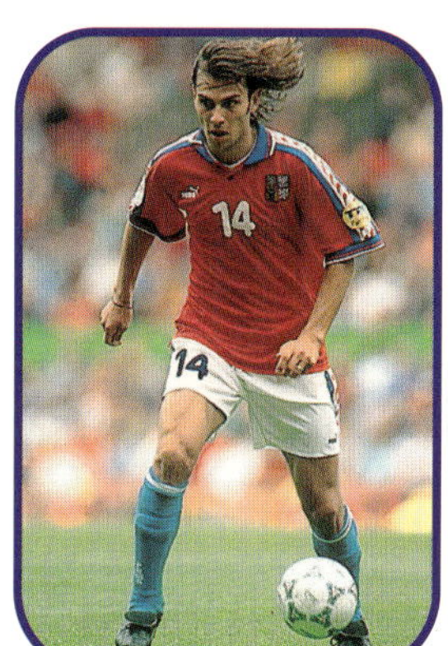

PLAY-OFF RESULTS

Scotland 0 England 2 (Scholes 2)
England 0 Scotland 1 (Hutchinson)
England win 2-1 on agg

Rep Ireland 1 (Robbie Keane) Turkey 1 (Tayfur, pen)
Turkey 0 Rep Ireland 0
Agg: 1-1; Turkey win on away goals.

Israel 0 Denmark 5 (Tomasson 2, Tofting, Jorgenson, Steen Nielsen)
Denmark 3 (Sand, Nielsen, Tomasson) Israel 0
Denmark win 8-0 on agg

Slovenia 2 (Zahovic, Acimovic) Ukraine 1 (Shevchenko)
Ukraine 1 (Rebrov, pen) Slovenia 1 (Pavlin)
Slovenia win 3-2 on agg

COME ON, ENGLAND